THE
EVERYTHING
VEGAN SLOW COOKER
COOKBOOK

Dear Reader,

We have a blended family in the Snyder house, but probably not in the way you think. Amy and the children are vegan and Justin is vegetarian, which means that most of what we cook is 100-percent free of animal products. That's why when we were given the opportunity to write an all-vegan cookbook, we just couldn't resist. Now we can share with readers some of our family's most enjoyed recipes using one of our favorite methods—the slow cooker.

The Everything® Vegan Slow Cooker Cookbook brings you 300 family-tested recipes straight from our kitchen. Even though our family skips animal products, our diets aren't heavy on mock meats and vegan cheeses, and our recipes aren't either. These occasional treats do make an appearance from time to time in this book, but you can easily omit them from many dishes. If you've never used a slow cooker, borrow one from a friend and try it out! By adding a slow cooker to your kitchen and cooking repertoire, you will save tons of time in the kitchen, which means more time for your loved ones.

We hope you enjoy!

Amy Snyder
Justin Snyder

Welcome to the EVERYTHING® Series!

These handy, accessible books give you all you need to tackle a difficult project, gain a new hobby, comprehend a fascinating topic, prepare for an exam, or even brush up on something you learned back in school but have since forgotten.

You can choose to read an Everything® book from cover to cover or just pick out the information you want from our four useful boxes: e-questions, e-facts, e-alerts, and e-ssentials. We give you everything you need to know on the subject, but throw in a lot of fun stuff along the way, too.

We now have more than 400 Everything® books in print, spanning such wide-ranging categories as weddings, pregnancy, cooking, music instruction, foreign language, crafts, pets, New Age, and so much more. When you're done reading them all, you can finally say you know Everything®!

QUESTION

Answers to
common questions

FACT

Important snippets
of information

ALERT

Urgent
warnings

ESSENTIAL

Quick
handy tips

PUBLISHER Karen Cooper

MANAGING EDITOR, EVERYTHING® SERIES Lisa Laing

COPY CHIEF Casey Ebert

ACQUISITIONS EDITOR Lisa Laing

DEVELOPMENT EDITOR Eileen Mullan

EVERYTHING® SERIES COVER DESIGNER Erin Alexander

LAYOUT DESIGNERS Erin Dawson, Jessica Faria, Michelle Roy Kelly, Elisabeth Lariviere

THE EVERYTHING®

VEGAN SLOW COOKER COOKBOOK

Amy Snyder and Justin Snyder

Authors of *The Everything Vegetarian® Slow Cooker Cookbook*

Avon, Massachusetts

For baby Rose, whom we can't wait to meet.

An Everything® Series Book.
Everything® and everything.com® are registered trademarks of F+W
Media, Inc.

Published by Adams Media, a division of F+W Media, Inc.
57 Littlefield Street, Avon, MA 02322 U.S.A.
www.adamsmedia.com

ISBN 10: 1-4405-4407-7
ISBN 13: 978-1-4405-4407-1
eISBN 10: 1-4405-4408-5
eISBN 13: 978-1-4405-4408-8

Printed in the United States of America.

10 9 8 7 6 5 4 3 2 1

Always follow safety and common-sense cooking protocol while using kitchen utensils, operating ovens and stoves, and handling uncooked food. If children are assisting in the preparation of any recipe, they should always be supervised by an adult.

This book is available at quantity discounts for bulk purchases.
For information, please call 1-800-289-0963.

Contents

Introduction

THE WORD *VEGAN* WAS coined in 1944, but the idea of not exploiting animals for food dates back much further, maybe even to the time of the Greek philosopher Pythagoras. Pythagoras was rumored to have been a vegetarian, and while this assumption still remains unproven, it is certainly true that if he did indeed forgo eating meat, it was not a popular choice like it is today. Animal rights was not a commonly discussed topic during this time and the wide variety of convenient vegan foods that we have today didn't exist. Fortunately, now it is not uncommon for people to know someone who is vegan, admire a vegan celebrity such as Ellen DeGeneres or Bill Clinton, or be vegan themselves!

Vegans do not eat meat, eggs, dairy, or any animal products, including honey. This differs from vegetarians, who still eat eggs and dairy products but avoid animal flesh, including fish. The reasons people go vegan are just as diverse as the people who choose the diet, but there are three reasons that are the most popular: to avoid cruelty to animals, the positive impact on the environment, and the many health benefits vegans enjoy.

Now on to the fun part: food! Vegan food has come a long way in recent years. While it was once a difficult undertaking to obtain vegan foods, it is now available in grocery stores and restaurants around the country, and there is even an abundance of online recipes and cookbooks to help you enjoy a vegan lifestyle. The quality of vegan food products is much higher, too, which makes it tastier and easier than ever to go vegan!

Vegan food can be prepared using all traditional cooking methods, but one of the methods that works best is slow cooking. Slow cookers usually require cooking a recipe over low heat for an extended period of time, which helps soften the sometimes tough vegan proteins—tempeh, seitan, and beans. Slow cooking also helps enhance flavors because of the long cooking time.

The Everything® Vegan Slow Cooker Cookbook brings you 300 easy vegan recipes that will tempt even the most hardcore meat eater. Think of vine-ripe tomatoes, fresh cloves of garlic, a drizzle of olive oil, and basil leaves simmering for hours until the flavors are intertwined. Or slices of tempeh that have been smothered in homemade barbecue sauce and slow cooked all day until they are melt-in-your-mouth soft at dinner time. The recipes in *The Everything® Vegan Slow Cooker Cookbook* combine local and worldly flavors using mostly fresh, all-natural ingredients instead of processed vegan substitutes. These do make an appearance in some recipes, but feel free to skip them if you would like.

Whether you are vegan, vegetarian, or just want to eat a little healthier from time to time, there's something for you in this book, so explore and enjoy!

CHAPTER 1

An Introduction to Slow Cookers and Veganism

There are many reasons to add more vegan recipes to your diet, from helping animals to eating food that is naturally cholesterol free, but the most delicious reason of all is that vegan food tastes good! And using a slow cooker to prepare healthy vegan recipes only makes it better. Slow cookers highlight the flavors in most recipes and help you achieve melt-in-your-mouth goodness. In addition, they also help you save time and energy in the kitchen, so it is a no-brainer to choose vegan slow cooker recipes!

All about Being Vegan

Vegan, sometimes called strict vegetarian, means someone who does not eat or use any animal products. This includes avoiding all meat, dairy, eggs, and honey, which differs from vegetarianism. Vegetarians typically eat dairy, eggs, and honey. Many vegans also choose not to wear any animal products such as silk, fur, leather, and wool. Instead, they wear natural materials like cotton and synthetic materials such as faux leather. Today, there are endless clothing options that do not contain a trace of animal products, and finding them at your local mall or stores such as Target and Walmart is easier than ever before.

Unfortunately, other products, such as household products and cosmetics, still involve animal cruelty. You may not realize that your bottle of shampoo or your dish soap was tested on an animal, but many are. Vegans avoid these products and those that contain animal ingredients. Packages aren't always clearly labeled, and it can take some practice deciphering all of the ingredients, but luckily, thanks to technology, there are mobile apps and lists that help make this easier.

This explains what vegans do, but you may still be wondering why?

QUESTION

What's wrong with eating honey?
Bees are often treated just like other animals that are used to make food. Farmers may take away the honey that bees need to stay alive during the winter, and when the bees are no longer profitable, they may be killed.

It Helps Animals

Billions of animals, including cows, pigs, and especially chickens, suffer because of the food industry each year. They don't spend their lives in idyllic pastures or in cute barns filled with bales of comfy hay. Instead, most animals raised to be consumed as food live out their lives in factory farms. On those factory farms, some animals are bred to grow so large that they cannot hold their own weight, and they may live out their days crammed into small, windowless spaces. There is little or no thought given to their well-being.

Many factory-farmed animals, including dairy cows and egg-laying chickens, live under these conditions. It's important to remember that products made by animals can contribute to an animal's suffering just as much as those products that are made from animals. Being vegan means that you avoid both of these types of products.

It's Good for Your Health

Recently, more people than ever are going vegan for their health, mind, and bodies, not just because of the cruelty to animals. Vegans, on average, weigh less than meat eaters, and they enjoy a reduced risk of heart disease and lower rates of diabetes. Additionally, vegans often report overall increased energy.

It's Good for the Environment

The 2006 United Nations report, "Livestock's Long Shadow," stated that "the livestock sector emerges as one of the top two or three most significant contributors to the most serious environmental problems, at every scale from local to global." Changing the way you eat can mean a greater change for the planet, even greater than carrying reusable bags or driving a hybrid car. Land degradation, climate change, air pollution, water shortage, and water pollution are just some of the damages done when animals are raised for food. You can help change this by leaving animals off your plate.

Advantages of a Vegan Diet

Going vegan won't make you look like your favorite Hollywood celebrity (who just might be vegan, too!) overnight, but with time you just might lose weight and improve your skin. Luckily, the advantages do not stop there, and there are many health benefits you'll experience by ditching meat, dairy, and eggs. Vegan diets are naturally:

- Low in calories
- Low in saturated fat
- Cholesterol free
- High in vitamins and minerals

Which means they are an excellent way to safeguard yourself against some unwanted diseases and weight gain.

Obesity

By skipping meat, dairy, and eggs when you eat, you are also skipping out on many unneeded calories in your diet. The average person needs roughly 2,000 calories per day, but most Americans are consuming far more than this. According to the Centers for Disease Control and Prevention, it is estimated that an alarming 36 percent of the population is now obese, and that number is only rising. Some people turn to diet pills or risky medical procedures for weight loss, but the solution can be much simpler—go vegan. While it is possible to be an obese vegan, because vegan foods are naturally lower in calories, it's not likely if you choose a healthy balanced diet.

Diabetes

In a 2009 position paper on vegetarian diets, the American Dietetic Association stated that vegetarians have lower rates of diabetes than their meat-eating counterparts, and by choosing a vegan diet, you can reduce the risk of and help treat diabetes even more. Since vegetarians and vegans are less likely to be overweight or obese, they are less likely to develop diabetes. There are also vitamins and nutrients, such as iron and fiber that are naturally present in vegan foods, that help reduce the risk of diabetes. The journal *Diabetes Care* includes a study which shows that consuming iron from animal sources *increases* the risk for diabetes, but when the source of iron is vegan, there is no such increase.

Heart Disease

A 1999 study published in the *American Journal of Clinical Nutrition* concluded that those who eat a cholesterol-free diet are over 50 percent less likely to develop heart disease than meat eaters (all animal products contain cholesterol), and there is little doubt surrounding the reason why. Since vegan diets are low in saturated fat and are totally free of cholesterol, saturated fat and cholesterol aren't present in the body to clog your arteries.

Of course, all decisions about your health should be discussed with a medical professional, and you should not embark on any treatment plans without your doctor's consent. Discuss veganism with your doctor and see if she recommends the diet for you.

How to Make the Switch

By now you may be thinking "I want to go vegan, but how do I make the switch?" Luckily, there are a plethora of resources (including this one!) out there to help you get started on your journey to a more compassionate lifestyle. You just need to decide which approach is best for you.

ESSENTIAL

There are two primary approaches to going vegan: cold turkey versus slowly easing in. Many people cannot eat another bite of nonvegan food once they learn about the conditions factory-farm-raised animals endure, but for others, the transition is not so easy. For those people, it is recommended that they slowly phase out meats, then eggs, and then dairy, piece by piece, and replace them with vegan alternatives instead. If this method will help you stick with a vegan diet in the long run, then go for it and don't beat yourself up about not being able to jump right in.

Research

As a new vegan, one of the first things you will want to do is figure out what you can and cannot eat. It will usually be pretty obvious (no more hamburgers and pork hot dogs!), but at times, it isn't so clear cut. PETA.org (*www.peta.org*) offers a list of ingredients that you may want to start looking out for when reading food labels. The names of these ingredients usually don't make it clear if a product is vegan or not. Don't obsess over getting this perfect though, and know that if trace amounts of animal products slip into your diet, you are still doing more good than harm overall. Personal purity does not have to be your ultimate goal when switching to a vegan diet.

Planning

A vegan diet doesn't take more time and planning than a meat-filled diet, but a healthy, balanced diet does. If you don't put some thought into nutrition, then chances are you are not going to be eating a healthy, balanced diet, regardless of whether you are a vegan or a meat eater. Vegans are often questioned about nutrition, though, and are most often asked about where they get their protein, iron, and calcium. These are all found naturally in a vegan diet. If you are concerned about getting enough of these substances, here is a quick guide to help you out.

- Protein: tofu, beans, quinoa
- Iron: beans, spinach, tempeh
- Calcium: collard greens, spinach, soybeans

Vegans are often concerned about vitamin B_{12}. This vitamin is not naturally found in plant-based foods, so you'll need to take a supplement. You can also choose foods such as soymilk and cereal that are fortified with all of these vitamins.

Experiment

Head out to your local grocery store, grab a cart, and start shopping, because experimenting with vegan food is the best part of becoming a vegan! Grocery store shelves are loaded with vegan cheeses, vegan mayonnaises, mock meats, and more. Most major grocery stores carry these products, but the store with the best options is Whole Foods. If you can't find the products you are looking for in the supermarket, head to the Internet. There are vegan food stores that deliver to your home!

Don't be afraid to try a recipe or ingredient you have not considered before. There are many cookbooks and websites to help you plan your new vegan menu. If you aren't exactly an at-home chef, head out to your local restaurants to start experimenting with vegan cuisine. You'll find a diverse number of options depending on where you live, how much you want to spend, and what your tastes are.

Benefits of Using a Slow Cooker

Slow cookers are affordable, easy to use, and fit comfortably on your countertop. After cooking a meal, you can simply remove the pot for cleaning, and put the slow cooker lid in a dishwasher or wash it by hand. Surprisingly, though, these aren't even the best reasons to choose a slow cooker for making your meals. The main reasons why slow cookers are a great choice for preparing delicious vegan recipes are because they're convenient, they save energy, and they are excellent at breaking down tough proteins.

Convenience

There are several benefits to slow cooking, but the one that is probably the most commonly cited is convenience. Many slow cooker recipes call for a long cooking time at a low temperature, and since the appliance does not require constant supervision, you are free to complete other tasks or even go to work while the meal is cooking. For busy parents, the appliance can be a time and life saver.

ALERT

All slow cookers are unique and come with their own set of instructions and warnings. Recommendations may be different based on the brand and size of the slow cooker. Be sure to read the information provided with your slow cooker carefully before getting started.

Most slow cooker recipes call for covering the pot with a lid, which means the liquid will not escape. This eliminates the risk of burning your food. Locking in the moisture like this also means that you don't have to constantly monitor your food as you would with stovetop cooking.

Energy Saver

When using a slow cooker, the energy saved is not just your own! This countertop appliance actually uses less electricity than an oven when preparing most recipes, and by reducing the energy used for cooking meals a few days a week, your kitchen will be a little greener. Using less electricity also means your wallet may end up being a little fatter, too, because of the savings you'll see with your utilities.

Tough Stuff

Slow cookers are often used to prepare recipes that call for cheaper cuts of meat because the longer cooking time helps soften the meat. While vegans don't eat meat, they can apply this information to cooking their protein staples: beans, tempeh, and seitan.

QUESTION

Can I cook dried beans in a slow cooker?
Dried beans may be prepared in a slow cooker, but you may want to first soak them overnight and boil the beans for 10 minutes before using them in recipes. This adds a fair amount of time to each recipe, so canned beans are often recommended instead.

Most slow cooker recipes call for enough liquid to submerge the main ingredients. Soaking tempeh in a warm liquid for an extended period of time helps soften and break down the dense protein made of fermented soybeans. Seitan isn't nearly as dense as tempeh, but it's also not very good at absorbing flavor. Slow cooking the seitan will help you avoid this obstacle.

Slow Cooking Tips and Tricks

Slow cookers are easy to use, but that doesn't mean a few tips and tricks won't help you achieve optimal results. And even a slow cooker veteran can use some handy reminders before firing up the slow cooker again. Here are a few tips to help you out:

- Recipes that call for a large quantity of liquid work best.
- The pot in your slow cooker should never be less than half full.

- The high setting is the same temperature as the low setting, food just reaches the simmer point faster.
- The lid should be used when operating a slow cooker.
- Stirring food during cooking is unnecessary.

As with any method of cooking, you won't find out what works best for your recipes until you try it. Use these tips to get yourself started or to help you troubleshoot problems you may be having with your slow cooker. If the problems continue, contact the manufacturer or try an Internet search to solve the problem. If all else fails, try the recipe again!

Adapting Recipes for Your Slow Cooker and Vegan Diet

Many recipes that were originally designed for an oven or stovetop can easily be adapted for just about any slow cooker. As long as you keep the main principles of slow cooking in mind—cooking ingredients in liquid, covered, for a long period of time—you shouldn't be afraid to experiment with other recipes that were not originally intended for a slow cooker.

ESSENTIAL

Whether you are cooking food in a slow cooker, the oven, or on the stove, the flavor of food will remain largely the same. Some methods highlight ingredients better than others, but for the most part, flavors don't change. Remember this when adapting recipes for your slow cooker.

Some cooking methods are easier to adapt for a slow cooker than others, though. For example, don't attempt to deep-fry food in a slow cooker on the low setting because the oil will not be hot enough to cook your food in a desirable way. Methods that call for cooking in a liquid, such as braising and stewing, are easiest for adapting to a slow cooker.

Slow cookers don't require exact cooking times or ingredient measurements like baking, which means you shouldn't be afraid to experiment! As long as you follow your slow cooker's instructions and use enough liquid to prevent burning, you're free to mix and match ingredients until you create recipes that work perfectly for your palette.

Your adventurous streak doesn't have to stop there. It's just as easy to adapt traditional recipes to a vegan diet. With these recipes, most of your ingredients will stay the same, except the protein and binding agents, such as eggs or cheese, will need to be replaced. Luckily, there are vegan substitutes for butter, cheese, milk, and a variety of meats available in grocery stores nationwide, and you can substitute most without any special instructions. As you become more comfortable with a vegan diet, try reducing the amount of imitation products you use in favor of healthier whole foods, such as tofu, tempeh, seitan, or beans. If you've never tried any of these ingredients, go ahead and add them to your favorite recipe to try out their interesting texture and get a vegan protein punch.

CHAPTER 2

Apps and Snacks

Spicy Seitan Buffalo Strips

*Most bottled buffalo wing sauces contain butter, so be sure to
read the label or make your own by following the steps below.*

INGREDIENTS | SERVES 6

⅓ cup Earth Balance Original Buttery
Spread

⅓ cup hot sauce

1 tablespoon vinegar

1 teaspoon garlic powder

2 (7-ounce) packages Gardein Chick'n
Strips

Serving Strips

Faux buffalo chicken strips can be added
to sandwiches or salads, but if you'd like to
serve them as an appetizer or snack, place
in a small basket lined with parchment
paper and add a side of celery sticks, carrot sticks, and vegan ranch.

1. Place the Earth Balance in a small bowl and
   microwave for 30 seconds, or until melted.

2. Add the hot sauce, vinegar, and garlic powder, and
   stir well.

3. In a 4-quart slow cooker, add the prepared hot sauce
   mixture and Chick'n Strips, and cook over low heat
   for 1 hour.

PER SERVING | Calories: 187 | Fat: 10 g | Protein: 17 g |
Sodium: 566 mg | Fiber: 1 g | Carbohydrates: 8 g | Sugar: 0 g

Mixed Veggie Dip

Try this vegetable-rich dip with pita chips or baked potato chips.

INGREDIENTS | SERVES 20

8 ounces vegan cream cheese, room temperature

½ cup vegan sour cream

½ teaspoon white pepper

½ teaspoon garlic powder

½ teaspoon onion powder

½ teaspoon vegan Worcestershire sauce

1 carrot, minced

1 stalk celery, minced

3 tablespoons minced, fresh spinach

¼ cup minced broccoli

1. In a 2-quart slow cooker, thoroughly mix all ingredients.

2. Cook on low for 2 hours. Stir before serving.

PER SERVING | Calories: 21 | Fat: 1.5 g | Protein: 1 g | Sodium: 14 mg | Fiber: 0 g | Carbohydrates: 1 g | Sugar: 1 g

Caramelized Onion Dip

Caramelized onions give this dip an amazing depth of flavor.

INGREDIENTS | SERVES 32

⅔ cup Caramelized Onions (see Chapter 7)

8 ounces vegan cream cheese

8 ounces vegan sour cream

1 tablespoon vegan Worcestershire sauce

¼ teaspoon white pepper

⅛ teaspoon flour

1. Place all ingredients into a 1½- or 2-quart slow cooker.

2. Heat on low for 2 hours. Whisk before serving.

PER SERVING (2 TABLESPOONS) | Calories: 20 | Fat: 2 g | Protein: 1 g | Sodium: 13 mg | Fiber: 0 g | Carbohydrates: 1 g | Sugar: 2 g

Barbecue "Meatballs"

Enjoy these "meatballs" as a two-bite snack, or use them as the filling in a hearty sub.

INGREDIENTS | SERVES 6

1 pound vegan ground beef, such as Gimme Lean Beef

½ onion, diced

1 clove garlic, minced

½ cup panko bread crumbs

1 (18-ounce) bottle barbecue sauce

Panko Bread Crumbs

Panko is a type of bread crumb made from white bread without crusts. It typically creates a crispier texture when used as the coating on food than regular bread crumbs. To make your own, bake crustless white bread crumbs until they are dry, but not browned.

1. In a large mixing bowl, combine the vegan ground beef, onion, garlic, and bread crumbs, and mix until well combined. (Using your hands is the easiest method.) Roll the "beef" mixture into 12 meatballs.

2. Add the "meatballs" to a 4-quart slow cooker.

3. Cover with barbecue sauce. Cover and cook over high heat for 1 hour.

PER SERVING (2 "MEATBALLS") | Calories: 268 | Fat: 4.5 g | Protein: 17 g | Sodium: 1,056 mg | Fiber: 1 g | Carbohydrates: 38 g | Sugar: 23 g

Baba Gannouj

Serve with toasted pita chips or as a vegetable dip.

INGREDIENTS | SERVES 6

1 tablespoon olive oil

1 large eggplant, peeled and diced

4 cloves garlic, peeled and minced

½ cup water

3 tablespoons fresh parsley

½ teaspoon salt

2 tablespoons fresh lemon juice

2 tablespoons tahini

1 tablespoon extra-virgin olive oil

1. In a 4-quart slow cooker, add the olive oil, eggplant, garlic, and water, and stir until coated. Cover and cook on high heat for 4 hours.

2. Strain the cooked eggplant and garlic and add to a food processor or blender along with the parsley, salt, lemon juice, and tahini. Pulse to process.

3. Scrape down the side of the food processor or blender container if necessary. Add the extra-virgin olive oil and process until smooth.

PER SERVING (½ CUP) | Calories: 24 | Fat: 2 g | Protein: 0.5 g | Sodium: 52 mg | Fiber: 1 g | Carbohydrates: 2 g | Sugar: 0.5 g

Cajun Peanuts

Use "green" raw peanuts, not cooked or dried nuts, to make this salty treat.

INGREDIENTS | SERVES 16

2 pounds raw peanuts
12 cups water
⅓ cup salt
1 (3-ounce) package crab boil seasoning

Crab Boil Seasoning

Crab boil seasoning is typically made from a combination of herbs and spices, such as red pepper flakes, black peppercorns, bay leaves, mustard seeds, coriander, and more. There are several brands of this flavorful blend available at grocery stores, including Zatarain's and Tony Chachere's.

1. Rinse the peanuts under cold water, and then place in a 6-quart slow cooker.

2. Add the water, salt, and crab boil. Cover and cook on high for 7 hours.

PER SERVING | Calories: 317 | Fat: 28 g | Protein: 14 g | Sodium: 2,373 mg | Fiber: 5 g | Carbohydrates: 9 g | Sugar: 2 g

Cinnamon and Sugar Peanuts

This is a festive treat that can be packaged in cellophane bags and given as party favors or gifts.

INGREDIENTS | SERVES 6

12 ounces unsalted, roasted peanuts
½ tablespoon ground cinnamon
⅓ cup sugar
1 tablespoon melted Earth Balance Original Buttery Spread

1. Place the peanuts in a 4-quart slow cooker.

2. Add the cinnamon and sugar, and drizzle with Earth Balance. Stir.

3. Cook on low, uncovered, for 2–3 hours, stirring occasionally.

4. Spread the peanut mixture onto a cookie sheet or parchment paper and cool until dry.

PER SERVING (1 OUNCE) | Calories: 200 | Fat: 15 g | Protein: 7 g | Sodium: 0 mg | Fiber: 2 g | Carbohydrates: 12 g | Sugar: 7 g

Zesty Lemon Hummus

Serve this zesty Middle Eastern spread with pita, vegetables, or falafel.

INGREDIENTS | SERVES 20

1 pound dried chickpeas
Water, as needed
3 tablespoons tahini
4 tablespoons lemon juice
Zest of 1 lemon
3 cloves garlic
¼ teaspoon salt

Easy Snacking

Keeping hummus and fresh vegetables around makes healthy snacking easy. Just cut carrots, celery, and radishes into snack-friendly sizes, and place them in a bowl with a tight fitting lid. Fill the bowl ⅔ with water. They will stay crisp in the refrigerator for up to 1 week.

1. In a 4-quart slow cooker, place the chickpeas and cover with water. Soak overnight, drain, and rinse. The next day, cook on low for 8 hours. Drain, reserving the liquid.

2. In a food processor, place the chickpeas, tahini, lemon juice, lemon zest, garlic, and salt. Pulse until smooth, adding the reserved liquid as needed to achieve the desired texture.

PER SERVING | Calories: 97 | Fat: 2.5 g | Protein: 5 g | Sodium: 38 mg | Fiber: 4 g | Carbohydrates: 15 g | Sugar: 2.5 g

Marinated Mushrooms and Garlic

Although white button mushrooms are most common, there are a variety of other exotic mushrooms, such as shiitake and chanterelles, that will work perfectly in this recipe.

INGREDIENTS | SERVES 6

2 (8-ounce) packages mushrooms
5 cloves garlic, minced
1 cup red wine
1 cup soy sauce
1 cup water
½ teaspoon tarragon
⅛ teaspoon salt
⅛ teaspoon black pepper

Add all ingredients to a 4-quart slow cooker, cover, and cook on medium heat for 3–4 hours.

PER SERVING | Calories: 76 | Fat: 0 g | Protein: 5 g | Sodium: 2,451 mg | Fiber: 1 g | Carbohydrates: 7 g | Sugar: 2 g

Southern Boiled Peanuts

On a warm summer day in the South, you can find roadside stands selling boiled peanuts by the bag full.

INGREDIENTS | SERVES 8

4 cups raw peanuts, rinsed
8 cups water
¼ cup kosher salt

Add all ingredients to a 4-quart slow cooker, cover, and cook on high heat for 5–6 hours. When the peanuts are tender, drain and serve.

PER SERVING | Calories: 413 | Fat: 35 g | Protein: 19 g | Sodium: 3,559 mg | Fiber: 6 g | Carbohydrates: 11.5 g | Sugar: 3 g

Kalamata Olive Hummus

This hummus can easily be spiced up with the addition of red pepper flakes.

INGREDIENTS | SERVES 6

1 pound dry chickpeas

7 cups water

⅓ cup tahini

2 lemons, juiced

¼ cup chopped kalamata olives

2 garlic cloves, minced

4 tablespoons olive oil

2 teaspoons cumin

¾ teaspoon salt

¼ teaspoon black pepper

1. Place the dry chickpeas and water in a 4-quart slow cooker, cover, and cook on high heat for 4 hours. Drain the chickpeas.

2. Combine the chickpeas and the rest of the ingredients in a food processor and purée until smooth.

PER SERVING | Calories: 296 | Fat: 18 g | Protein: 9 g | Sodium: 325 mg | Fiber: 8 g | Carbohydrates: 27 g | Sugar: 4 g

Protein Punch

Hummus is a great source of protein and iron, making it an excellent choice for vegans. Even little ones love the creamy treat!

Spinach and Artichoke Dip

*The easiest way to drain thawed spinach is to grab a small handful
and squeeze it in your hands until all the water is wrung out.*

INGREDIENTS | SERVES 6

2 tablespoons Earth Balance Original Buttery Spread

½ onion, diced

1 garlic clove, minced

2 teaspoons flour

2 cups unsweetened almond milk

1 lemon, juiced

1 (1-pound) bag frozen spinach, thawed, with water squeezed out

1 (14-ounce) can artichokes, drained and chopped

⅛ teaspoon nutmeg

⅛ teaspoon salt

⅛ teaspoon black pepper

1. Add the Earth Balance to the slow cooker, and sauté the onion and garlic on medium heat for 3–4 minutes. Stir in the flour until the mixture is smooth.

2. Add the remaining ingredients, stir, cover, and cook on medium heat for 2–3 hours.

PER SERVING | Calories: 140 | Fat: 8 g | Protein: 6 g | Sodium: 252 mg | Fiber: 7 g | Carbohydrates: 18 g | Sugar: 5 g

Creamy Cilantro Dip

This versatile dip can be served with tortilla chips, pita wedges, vegetables, or as a sandwich condiment.

INGREDIENTS | SERVES 6

½ pound dry white beans

3¼ cups water

1 bunch cilantro, washed and stemmed

1 tablespoon olive oil

1 lime, juiced

½ teaspoon salt

⅛ teaspoon black pepper

Cilantrophobia

You either love it or you hate it, and those who hate cilantro *really* hate it. Studies suggest that the aversion to the green leafy herb may be genetic, but it's still largely unknown why some people can't stomach the herb that is described as tasting like soap.

1. Place the dry white beans and 3 cups water in a 4-quart slow cooker, cover, and cook on high heat for 4–5 hours, or until the beans are tender. Drain the white beans.

2. While the beans are cooking, purée the cilantro, olive oil, lime juice, salt, and pepper in a food processor. Set the herb mixture aside in a small bowl.

3. Add the drained white beans and ¼ cup of water to the food processor, and purée until it reaches a smooth consistency.

4. In a large bowl, combine the white beans and the herb mixture. Cover and chill for 2 hours before serving.

PER SERVING | Calories: 155 | Fat: 3 g | Protein: 8 g | Sodium: 220 mg | Fiber: 8 g | Carbohydrates: 25 g | Sugar: 3.6 g

Teriyaki Veggie Skewers

If you are using an oval slow cooker or one that is very large, save time by prepping the skewers the night before cooking and storing in the fridge.

INGREDIENTS | SERVES 4

1 red bell pepper, cut into 16 (1-inch) chunks

1 eggplant, cut into 16 large chunks

1 pineapple, peeled and cut into 16 large chunks

1 tablespoon vegetable oil

¼ cup soy sauce

1 cup water

⅓ cup brown sugar

1 tablespoon grated, fresh ginger

2 cloves garlic, minced

1 package of 6-inch skewers

1. In a large mixing bowl, toss the red bell pepper, eggplant, and pineapple with the vegetable oil.

2. In a small bowl, whisk the soy sauce, water, brown sugar, ginger, and garlic together.

3. Add all the ingredients to a 4-quart slow cooker, cover, and cook on medium-high heat for 3–4 hours.

4. Assemble the skewers with the bell pepper, eggplant, and pineapple, then repeat bell pepper, eggplant, and pineapple.

PER SERVING | Calories: 266 | Fat: 4 g | Protein: 4 g | Sodium: 911 mg | Fiber: 8.5 g | Carbohydrates: 60 g | Sugar: 44 g

Sweet Beet Dip

Beets have another culinary use aside from being eaten. They can be used as red or pink vegan-friendly food coloring.

INGREDIENTS | SERVES 6

6 large beets, peeled and quartered

½ cup apple juice

½ cup orange juice

1 teaspoon red wine vinegar

¼ teaspoon salt

⅛ teaspoon black pepper

1. Add all ingredients to a 4-quart slow cooker, cover, and cook on medium-high heat for 5–6 hours, or until the beets are tender.

2. Purée the beets in a food processor or blender, adding just enough of the liquid to create a smooth consistency. Serve cold or at room temperature.

PER SERVING | Calories: 55 | Fat: 0 g | Protein: 1.4 g | Sodium: 163 mg | Fiber: 2.5 g | Carbohydrates: 12 g | Sugar: 9 g

Beet Greens

Don't toss the tops! The greens at the top of beets can be cooked and eaten, too. Sauté them in some olive oil and season with salt and pepper.

Cranberry Jalapeño Relish

If you can't take the heat, leave the jalapeños out of this recipe for a more traditional relish.

INGREDIENTS | SERVES 6

1 (12-ounce) bag frozen cranberries

2 oranges, juiced

1 lemon, juiced

1 cup sugar

1 jalapeño, minced

2 tablespoons water

¼ teaspoon salt

¼ black pepper

Add all ingredients to a 4-quart slow cooker, stir, cover, and cook on medium heat for 2–3 hours.

PER SERVING | Calories: 179 | Fat: 0 g | Protein: 1 g | Sodium: 100 mg | Fiber: 4 g | Carbohydrates: 46 g | Sugar: 40 g

Edamame-Miso Dip

The Asian flavors of this unique dip are both subtle and satisfying.

INGREDIENTS | SERVES 4

½ pound frozen shelled edamame

3 cups water

1 tablespoon soy sauce

2½ tablespoons miso paste

2 green onions, thinly sliced

⅛ teaspoon salt

1. Add all ingredients to a 4-quart slow cooker, stir, cover, and cook on low heat for 2 hours, or until the edamame is tender.

2. Using a slotted spoon, remove the edamame and place it in a food processor or blender. Purée the edamame, adding enough of the cooking liquid to create a smooth consistency. Serve cold or at room temperature.

PER SERVING | Calories: 86 | Fat: 4 g | Protein: 7 g | Sodium: 312 mg | Fiber: 2.4 g | Carbohydrates: 7 g | Sugar: 0 g

Parsley and Thyme White Bean Dip

Don't substitute fresh herbs with the dried variety in this recipe. Fresh herbs are needed to complement the lemon and give the dip a light and refreshing flavor.

INGREDIENTS | SERVES 6

2 tablespoons olive oil

½ onion, diced

3 cloves garlic, minced

½ pound dry white beans

3 cups water

1 lemon, juiced

1 tablespoon chopped, fresh parsley

½ tablespoon fresh thyme

¼ teaspoon salt

⅛ teaspoon black pepper

Storing Bean Dips

Dried beans take a while to cook, so to save time in the kitchen you can make a large batch of your favorite bean dip and then freeze the unused portions. Place the desired amount in a freezer-safe bag, label, and store for up to 3 months.

1. Add the olive oil to the slow cooker and sauté the onion and garlic on medium-high heat for 3–4 minutes. Add the dry white beans and 3 cups water to the slow cooker. Cover and cook on high heat for 4–5 hours, or until the beans are tender. Drain the white beans.

2. In a food processor, purée the white beans, adding enough water to create a smooth consistency. Add the lemon juice, parsley, thyme, salt, and pepper, and continue to blend until very smooth.

3. Cover and refrigerate for at least 2 hours before serving.

PER SERVING | Calories: 175 | Fat: 5 g | Protein: 8 g | Sodium: 109 mg | Fiber: 7.5 g | Carbohydrates: 26 g | Sugar: 4 g

Pintos, Cerveza, and Lime Dip

If you don't have a Mexican beer on hand, a domestic beer will work just fine.

INGREDIENTS | SERVES 6

2 tablespoons olive oil

½ onion, diced

3 cloves garlic, minced

½ pound dry pinto beans

3 cups water

1 (12-ounce) Mexican beer

1 fresh jalapeño, minced

2 limes, juiced

¼ teaspoon, salt

⅛ teaspoon, black pepper

1. Add the olive oil to the slow cooker and sauté the onion and garlic on medium-high heat for 3–4 minutes.

2. Add the dry pinto beans, 3 cups water, and beer to the slow cooker. Cover and cook on high heat for 4–5 hours, or until the beans are tender. Drain the pinto beans.

3. In a food processor, purée the pinto beans, minced jalapeño, lime juice, salt, and pepper, adding enough water to create a smooth consistency. Serve hot or at room temperature.

PER SERVING | Calories: 109 | Fat: 5 g | Protein: 2.5 g | Sodium: 214 mg | Fiber: 2.5 g | Carbohydrates: 11.5 g | Sugar: 1 g

Garlic Confit

Use this garlic in place of fresh garlic in appropriate recipes,
or you can enjoy it smashed and spread on toasted bread.

INGREDIENTS | YIELDS 5 HEADS OF GARLIC

3 cups olive oil

5 heads of garlic, with cloves peeled

3 dried red chilies

Preserving Garlic

Garlic confit is a great and easy way to preserve garlic when it is in season and at its peak. Garlic prepared using this method can be jarred and stored for up to 3 months.

1. Add all ingredients to a 4-quart slow cooker. Make sure there is enough oil to cover all the garlic cloves. Place the cover on the slow cooker and cook on low heat for 4 hours, or until the garlic is tender.

2. Remove the garlic with a slotted spoon and place in canning jars. Pour the oil over the garlic and seal the top.

PER SERVING (¼ HEAD) | Calories: 305 | Fat: 32 g | Protein: 1 g | Sodium: 3 mg | Fiber: 0 g | Carbohydrates: 4 g | Sugar: 0.5 g

CHAPTER 3

Soups

Tofu Noodle Soup

*Even firm tofu is quite soft, so for added texture,
freeze the tofu and bake before adding to the soup.*

INGREDIENTS | SERVES 4

2 tablespoons olive oil

1 medium onion, diced

3 cloves garlic, minced

2 ribs celery, sliced in ½-inch pieces

7 ounces extra-firm tofu, cubed

5 cups Vegetable Broth (see recipe in this chapter)

1 bay leaf

1 teaspoon salt

1 lemon, juiced

2 teaspoons chopped, fresh parsley

2 teaspoons chopped, fresh thyme

8 ounces cooked egg noodles or linguine

1. In a large sauté pan heat the olive oil over medium heat. Add the onion, garlic, and celery, and sauté for 3 minutes.

2. Add the tofu and cook 5 additional minutes.

3. In a 4-quart slow cooker, pour the sautéed vegetables, tofu, Vegetable Broth, bay leaf, and salt. Cover and cook on low for 8 hours.

4. Add the lemon juice, parsley, thyme, and pasta. Cover and cook for an additional 20 minutes.

PER SERVING | Calories: 401 | Fat: 9 g | Protein: 14 g | Sodium: 612 mg | Fiber: 9 g | Carbohydrates: 66 g | Sugar: 13 g

Herbal Options

A variety of herbs can work well in Tofu Noodle Soup. Try substituting basil, rosemary, or even dill in this recipe.

Hot and Sour Soup

Adjust the spiciness of this soup by adding more or less chili paste, to taste.

INGREDIENTS | SERVES 6

4 cups Vegetable Broth (see recipe in this chapter)

2 tablespoons soy sauce

2 tablespoons rice vinegar

1 teaspoon sesame oil

2 ounces dried Chinese mushrooms

½ cup sliced canned bamboo shoots

4 ounces extra-firm tofu, cubed

1 tablespoon red chili paste

1 teaspoon white pepper

2 tablespoons cornstarch mixed with ¼ cup water

1. In a 4-quart slow cooker, add all ingredients except for the cornstarch mixture. Cook on low for 6 hours.

2. Pour in the cornstarch mixture, stir, and cook on high heat for 20 additional minutes.

PER SERVING | Calories: 76 | Fat: 1.5 g | Protein: 3 g | Sodium: 396 mg | Fiber: 3 g | Carbohydrates: 13 g | Sugar: 5 g

Vegetable Broth

A versatile vegetable broth can be used as the base for almost any soup or stew. Note that it does not contain salt, so you must add that separately when using this broth in recipes.

INGREDIENTS | YIELDS 4 CUPS

2 large onions, peeled and halved

2 medium carrots, cleaned and cut into large pieces

3 stalks celery, cut in half

1 whole bulb garlic, crushed

10 peppercorns

1 bay leaf

6 cups water

1. Add all ingredients to a 4-quart slow cooker. Cover and cook on low heat for 8–10 hours.

2. Strain the broth to remove the vegetables. Store in the refrigerator.

PER SERVING (1 CUP) | Calories: 42 | Fat: 0 g | Protein: 1 g | Sodium: 62 mg | Fiber: 2 g | Carbohydrates: 9.5 g | Sugar: 4.5 g

Storing Broth

Homemade broth can be stored in a covered container in the refrigerator for 2–3 days, or frozen for up to 3 months.

Cauliflower Soup

Cauliflower's peak season is the fall, so try this soup on a crisp autumn night.

INGREDIENTS | SERVES 6

1 small head cauliflower, chopped
½ onion, diced
1 teaspoon salt
1 teaspoon pepper
2 tablespoons Earth Balance Original Buttery Spread
4 cups Vegetable Broth (see recipe in this chapter)
Zest of ½ lemon

1. In a 4-quart slow cooker, add all ingredients. Cover and cook on low for 6 hours.

2. Turn off slow cooker and let soup cool about 10 minutes. Using a blender or immersion blender, process until very smooth.

3. Return soup to the slow cooker and add lemon zest. Heat until warm.

PER SERVING | Calories: 98 | Fat: 4 g | Protein: 3 g | Sodium: 474 mg | Fiber: 4 g | Carbohydrates: 14 g | Sugar: 6 g

Zest Versus Juice

Lemon zest is obtained by grating the outer peel of the lemon. It contains a more intense lemon flavor than the juice of the citrus fruit, although many recipes call for both lemon zest and lemon juice.

Red Lentil Soup

*Store-bought vegetable broth or stock typically contains much more sodium
than the homemade variety, so adjust salt accordingly.*

INGREDIENTS | SERVES 6

3 tablespoons olive oil

1 small onion, sliced

1½ teaspoons peeled and minced fresh ginger

2 cloves garlic, minced

2 cups red lentils

6 cups Vegetable Broth (see recipe in this chapter)

1 lemon, juiced

½ teaspoon paprika

1 teaspoon cayenne pepper

1½ teaspoons salt

1. In a sauté pan, heat the olive oil over medium heat, then sauté the onion, ginger, and garlic for 2–3 minutes.

2. In a 4-quart slow cooker, add the sautéed vegetables and all remaining ingredients. Cover and cook on low for 6–8 hours. Add more salt, if necessary, to taste.

PER SERVING | Calories: 296 | Fat: 8 g | Protein: 18 g | Sodium: 594 mg | Fiber: 8 g | Carbohydrates: 54 g | Sugar: 8 g

Cleaning Lentils

Before cooking lentils, rinse them carefully by placing in a colander and running ample cold water over them. Sort through the bunch to remove any debris that may be lingering behind and discard.

Black Bean Soup

You can use the leftover green bell pepper, red bell pepper, and red onion from this recipe to make Fajita Chili (see Chapter 5).

INGREDIENTS | SERVES 6

2 tablespoons olive oil

½ green bell pepper, diced

½ red bell pepper, diced

½ red onion, sliced

2 cloves garlic, minced

2 (15-ounce) cans black beans, drained and rinsed

2 teaspoons minced cumin

1 teaspoon chipotle powder

1 teaspoon salt

4 cups Vegetable Broth (see recipe in this chapter)

¼ cup chopped cilantro

1. In a sauté pan, heat the olive oil over medium heat, then sauté the bell peppers, onion, and garlic for 2–3 minutes.

2. In a 4-quart slow cooker, add the sautéed vegetables, black beans, cumin, chipotle powder, salt, and Vegetable Broth. Cover and cook on low for 6 hours.

3. Let the soup cool slightly, and then pour half into a blender. Process until smooth, then pour back into the pot. Add the chopped cilantro and stir.

PER SERVING | Calories: 204 | Fat: 6 g | Protein: 9 g | Sodium: 865 mg | Fiber: 10 g | Carbohydrates: 31 g | Sugar: 7 g

Potato-Leek Soup

If you'd like to omit the alcohol from this recipe, just add another ½ cup of Vegetable Broth.

INGREDIENTS | SERVES 6

2 tablespoons Earth Balance Original Buttery Spread

2 small leeks, chopped (white and light green parts only)

3 large russet potatoes, peeled and diced

4 cups Vegetable Broth (see recipe in this chapter)

½ cup white wine

½ cup water

1 teaspoon salt

1 teaspoon pepper

¼ teaspoon dried thyme

1. In a sauté pan over medium heat, melt the Earth Balance, then add the leeks. Cook until softened, about 5 minutes.

2. In a 4-quart slow cooker, add the sautéed leeks, potatoes, broth, wine, water, salt, pepper, and thyme. Cover and cook over low heat 6–8 hours.

3. Allow soup to cool slightly, then use an immersion blender or traditional blender to process until smooth.

PER SERVING | Calories: 177 | Fat: 4 g | Protein: 3 g | Sodium: 459 mg | Fiber: 5 g | Carbohydrates: 29 g | Sugar: 6 g

Pumpkin-Ale Soup

Use fresh pumpkin in place of the canned pumpkin purée when the ingredient is in season. You'll need 3¾ cup of cooked, puréed fresh pumpkin.

INGREDIENTS | SERVES 6

2 (15-ounce) cans pumpkin purée

¼ cup diced onion

2 cloves garlic, minced

2 teaspoons salt

1 teaspoon pepper

¼ teaspoon dried thyme

5 cups Vegetable Broth (see recipe in this chapter)

1 (12-ounce) bottle pale ale beer

1. In a 4-quart slow cooker, add the pumpkin purée, onion, garlic, salt, pepper, thyme, and Vegetable Broth. Stir well. Cover and cook over low heat for 4 hours.

2. Allow the soup to cool slightly, then process in a blender or with an immersion blender until smooth.

3. Pour the soup back into the slow cooker, add the beer, and cook for 1 hour over low heat.

PER SERVING | Calories: 108 | Fat: 0 g | Protein: 3 g | Sodium: 795 mg | Fiber: 3 g | Carbohydrates: 22 g | Sugar: 7 g

Butternut Squash Soup

You can substitute an extra cup of Vegetable Broth for the white wine in this soup.

INGREDIENTS | SERVES 6

1 medium butternut squash, peeled and diced

1 russet potato, peeled and diced

1 large carrot, chopped

1 rib celery, sliced

1 onion, diced

4 cups Vegetable Broth (see recipe in this chapter)

1 cup white wine

1 bay leaf

¼ teaspoon dried thyme

1½ teaspoons salt

¼ teaspoon nutmeg

1. Add all of the ingredients to a 4-quart slow cooker. Cover and cook over low heat for 6 hours.

2. Cool the soup slightly, then remove the bay leaf. Process in a blender or using an immersion blender.

PER SERVING | Calories: 115 | Fat: 0 g | Protein: 3 g | Sodium: 687 mg | Fiber: 4.5 g | Carbohydrates: 20 g | Sugar: 7 g

Vegetable Cuts

When chopping vegetables for a dish that will be blended, save time by not trying to make them too perfect or too small.

Tomato Basil Soup

*Fresh basil adds a different flavor to dishes than dried basil,
and the fresh variety is more complementary to this soup.*

INGREDIENTS | SERVES 5

2 tablespoons Earth Balance Original Buttery Spread

½ onion, diced

2 cloves garlic, minced

1 (28-ounce) can whole peeled tomatoes

½ cup Vegetable Broth (see recipe in this chapter)

1 bay leaf

1 teaspoon salt

1 teaspoon pepper

½ cup unsweetened soymilk

¼ cup sliced, fresh basil

1. In a sauté pan over medium heat, melt the Earth Balance, then sauté the onion and garlic for 3–4 minutes.

2. In a 4-quart slow cooker, add the onion and garlic, tomatoes, Vegetable Broth, bay leaf, salt, and pepper. Cover and cook over low heat 4 hours.

3. Allow to cool slightly, then remove the bay leaf. Process the soup in a blender or immersion blender.

4. Return the soup to the slow cooker, then add the soymilk and chopped basil; heat on low for an additional 30 minutes.

PER SERVING | Calories: 95 | Fat: 5.5 g | Protein: 3 g | Sodium: 501 mg | Fiber: 3 g | Carbohydrates: 10.5 g | Sugar: 6 g

Creamy Chickpea Soup

Almost any bean can be puréed to make a creamy soup without the cream, but chickpeas work especially well.

INGREDIENTS | SERVES 6

1 small onion, diced

2 cloves garlic, minced

2 (15-ounce) cans chickpeas, drained and rinsed

5 cups Vegetable Broth (see recipe in this chapter)

1 teaspoon salt

½ teaspoon cumin

Juice of ½ lemon

1 tablespoon olive oil

¼ cup chopped, fresh parsley

1. In a 4-quart slow cooker, add all ingredients except for the lemon juice, olive oil, and parsley. Cover and cook over low heat for 4 hours.

2. Allow to cool slightly, then process the soup in a blender or using an immersion blender.

3. Return the soup to the slow cooker and add the lemon juice, olive oil, and parsley. Heat on low for an additional 30 minutes.

PER SERVING | Calories: 205 | Fat: 11 g | Protein: 7 g | Sodium: 403 mg | Fiber: 6.5 g | Carbohydrates: 33 g | Sugar: 0.5 g

Minestrone Soup

Minestrone is a classic Italian vegetable soup. The zucchini and cabbage are added at the end for a burst of fresh flavor.

INGREDIENTS | SERVES 8

3 cloves garlic, minced

15 ounces canned fire-roasted diced tomatoes

28 ounces canned crushed tomatoes

2 stalks celery, diced

1 medium onion, diced

3 medium carrots, diced

3 cups Vegetable Broth (see recipe in this chapter)

30 ounces canned kidney beans, drained and rinsed

2 tablespoons tomato paste

2 tablespoons minced basil

2 tablespoons minced oregano

2 tablespoons minced Italian parsley

1½ cups shredded cabbage

¾ cup diced zucchini

1 teaspoon salt

½ teaspoon pepper

8 ounces small cooked pasta

1. In a 4-quart slow cooker, add the garlic, diced and crushed tomatoes, celery, onions, carrots, broth, beans, tomato paste, basil, oregano, and parsley. Cover and cook on low heat for 6–8 hours.

2. Add shredded cabbage and zucchini, and turn to high for the last hour.

3. Stir in the salt, pepper, and pasta before serving.

PER SERVING | Calories: 470 | Fat: 1.5 g | Protein: 28 g | Sodium: 320 mg | Fiber: 21 g | Carbohydrates: 89 g | Sugar: 11.5 g

Suggested Pasta Shapes for Soup

Anchellini, small shells, hoops, alfabeto, or ditaletti are all small pasta shapes suitable for soup. For heartier soups, try bow ties or rotini. Thin rice noodles or vermicelli are better for Asian-style soups.

Mushroom Barley Soup

Using three types of mushrooms in this soup adds a robust, earthy flavor.

INGREDIENTS | SERVES 8

1 ounce dried porcini mushrooms

1 cup boiling water

1½ teaspoons Earth Balance Original Buttery Spread

5 ounces fresh shiitake mushrooms, sliced

4 ounces fresh button mushrooms, sliced

1 large onion, diced

1 clove garlic, minced

⅔ cup medium pearl barley

¼ teaspoon ground black pepper

½ teaspoon salt

6 cups Vegetable Broth (see recipe in this chapter)

1. Place the dried porcini mushrooms in a heat-safe bowl. Pour the boiling water over the mushrooms. Soak for 15 minutes.

2. Meanwhile, in a sauté pan, melt the Earth Balance over medium heat. Sauté the fresh mushrooms, onion, and garlic until the onions are soft, about 3 minutes.

3. Drain the porcini mushrooms and discard the water.

4. In a 4-quart slow cooker, add all of the mushrooms, onions, garlic, barley, pepper, salt, and the broth. Stir, cover, and cook 6–8 hours on low.

PER SERVING | Calories: 117 | Fat: 1 g | Protein: 4 g | Sodium: 210 mg | Fiber: 5.5 g | Carbohydrates: 24 g | Sugar: 6 g

Summer Borscht

Serve this cooling soup with a dollop of vegan sour cream, such as Tofutti Sour Supreme.

INGREDIENTS | SERVES 6

3½ cups shredded cooked beets

¼ cup diced onion

½ teaspoon salt

1 teaspoon sugar

¼ cup lemon juice

½ tablespoon celery seed

2 cups Vegetable Broth (see recipe in this chapter)

2 cups water

1. Place all of the ingredients in a 4-quart slow cooker. Cover and cook on low for 6–8 hours or on high for 4 hours.

2. Refrigerate the soup for 4 hours or overnight. Serve cold.

PER SERVING | Calories: 60 | Fat: 0.5 g | Sodium: 287.5 mg | Carbohydrates: 14 g | Fiber: 4 g | Protein: 2 g | Sugar: 8 g

Can't Beat Beets

Beets, also known as beetroot, can be peeled, steamed, cooked, pickled, and shredded. They are good hot or cold, and they are high in folate, vitamin C, potassium, and fiber. Although they have the highest sugar content of all vegetables, beets are very low in calories. One beet is only 75 calories.

Tortilla Soup

Turn this soup into a complete meal by adding pieces of cooked vegan chicken, such as Morningstar Farms Meal Starters Chik'n Strips or Gardein Seasoned Bites.

INGREDIENTS | SERVES 8

2 tablespoons olive oil

1 large onion, chopped

2 cloves garlic, minced

2 tablespoons soy sauce

7 cups Vegetable Broth (see recipe in this chapter)

12 ounces firm silken tofu, crumbled

2 cups diced tomato

1 cup corn kernels

1 teaspoon chipotle powder

1 teaspoon cayenne pepper

2 teaspoons ground cumin

2 teaspoons salt

1 teaspoon dried oregano

10 small corn tortillas, sliced

8 ounces shredded vegan cheese, such as Daiya Mozzarella Style Shreds

Chipotle Powder

Chipotle powder is made from ground chipotle peppers, a type of dried jalapeño. It brings a smoky spiciness to dishes, but it can be replaced with cayenne pepper or chili powder.

1. In a sauté pan over medium heat, add the olive oil. Sauté the onions until just soft, about 3 minutes. Add the garlic and sauté for an additional 30 seconds.

2. In a 4-quart slow cooker, add all ingredients except tortillas and cheese. Stir, cover, and cook over low heat for 4 hours.

3. While the soup is cooking, preheat oven to 450°F. Slice the corn tortillas into thin strips and place them on an ungreased baking sheet. Bake for about 10 minutes, or until they turn golden brown. Remove from heat and set aside.

4. After the soup has cooled slightly, use an immersion blender or regular blender to purée the soup.

5. Serve with baked tortilla strips and 1 ounce shredded cheese in each bowl of soup.

PER SERVING | Calories: 298 | Fat: 15 g | Protein: 14 g | Sodium: 1,043 mg | Fiber: 4.5 g | Carbohydrates: 29 g | Sugar: 5 g

Greek-Style Orzo and Spinach Soup

Lemon zest adds a bright, robust flavor to this simple soup.

INGREDIENTS | SERVES 6

2 cloves garlic, minced

3 tablespoons lemon juice

1 teaspoon lemon zest

5 cups Vegetable Broth (see recipe in this chapter)

1½ teaspoons salt

1 small onion, thinly sliced

1 package extra-firm tofu, cubed

4 cups fresh baby spinach

⅓ cup dried orzo

1. In a 4-quart slow cooker, add the garlic, lemon juice, zest, broth, salt, onion, tofu, and spinach. Cover and cook on low for 1 hour.

2. Add the orzo, stir, and continue to cook on high for an additional 15 minutes. Stir before serving.

PER SERVING | Calories: 87 | Fat: 3 g | Protein: 9 g | Sodium: 647 mg | Fiber: 1 g | Carbohydrates: 7 g | Sugar: 2 g

Quick Tip: Zesting

There are many tools on the market that are for zesting citrus, but all you really need is a fine grater. Be sure to take off the outermost part of the peel, where the aromatic essential oils that hold the flavor are located. The white pith underneath is bitter and inedible.

Pho

This Vietnamese noodle soup is easy to make in the slow cooker.
Try it instead of vegetable soup on a cold night.

INGREDIENTS | SERVES 6

1 tablespoon coriander seeds

1 tablespoon whole cloves

6 star anise

1 cinnamon stick

1 tablespoon fennel seed

1 tablespoon whole cardamom

4 knobs fresh ginger, sliced

1 onion, sliced

1 quart Vegetable Broth (see recipe in this chapter)

1 teaspoon soy sauce

8 ounces Vietnamese rice noodles

1 cup shredded seitan

½ cup chopped cilantro

½ cup chopped Thai basil

2 cups mung bean sprouts

¼ cup sliced scallions

1. In a dry nonstick skillet, quickly heat the spices, ginger, and onion over high heat until the seeds start to pop, about 5 minutes. The onion and ginger should look slightly caramelized. Place in a cheesecloth packet and tie it securely.

2. In a 4-quart slow cooker, place the cheesecloth packet. Add the broth, soy sauce, noodles, and seitan. Cover, and cook on low for 4 hours.

3. Remove the cheesecloth packet after cooking. Serve each bowl topped with cilantro, basil, sprouts, and scallions.

PER SERVING | Calories: 267 | Fat: 12 g | Protein: 7 g | Sodium: 272 mg | Fiber: 5 g | Carbohydrates: 36 g | Sugar: 5 g

French Onion Soup

Vidalia onions are a sweet variety of onion that work particularly well in this French Onion Soup.

INGREDIENTS | SERVES 4

¼ cup olive oil

4 Vidalia onions, sliced

4 cloves garlic, minced

1 tablespoon dried thyme

1 cup red wine

4 cups Vegetable Broth (see recipe in this chapter)

1 teaspoon salt

1 teaspoon pepper

4 slices French bread

4 ounces vegan cheese such as Daiya Mozzarella Style Shreds

1. In a sauté pan, heat the olive oil over medium-high heat and cook the onions until golden brown, about 3 minutes. Add the garlic and sauté for 1 minute.

2. In a 4-quart slow cooker, pour the sautéed vegetables, thyme, red wine, broth, salt, and pepper. Cover and cook on low heat for 4 hours.

3. While the soup is cooking, preheat the oven to the broiler setting. Lightly toast the slices of French bread.

4. To serve, ladle the soup into a broiler-safe bowl, place a slice of the toasted French bread on top of the soup, sprinkle the vegan cheese on top of the bread, and place the soup under the broiler until the cheese has melted.

PER SERVING | Calories: 471 | Fat: 22 g | Protein: 14 g | Sodium: 859 g | Fiber: 6 g | Carbohydrates: 45 g | Sugar: 12 g

Celery Root Soup

Serve a bowl of this soup topped with green apple crisps.

INGREDIENTS | SERVES 6

2 tablespoons Earth Balance Original Buttery Spread

1 small leek (white and light green parts only), chopped

2 cloves garlic, minced

1 large celery root, peeled and cubed

2 medium russet potatoes, peeled and cubed

6 cups Vegetable Broth (see recipe in this chapter)

1½ teaspoons salt

1 teaspoon pepper

1. In a large sauté pan over medium heat, melt the Earth Balance, then add the leeks and sauté about 4 minutes. Add the garlic and sauté an additional 30 seconds.

2. In a 4-quart slow cooker, add the sautéed leeks and garlic, celery root, potatoes, broth, salt, and pepper. Cover and cook over low heat for 6–8 hours.

3. Let the soup cool slightly, then process in a blender or with an immersion blender until smooth.

PER SERVING | Calories: 147.5 | Fat: 4 g | Protein: 3 g | Sodium: 679 mg | Fiber: 5 g | Carbohydrates: 26 g | Sugar: 7 g

Celery Root

Celery root, also known as celeriac, is not the root of the celery you know. It is similar in texture to a potato and is cultivated for its root, not its leaves or stalk. It is grown in cool weather and is best in the fall, right after it has been pulled. The roots and crevices have to be trimmed away, so a 1-pound root will only yield about 2 cups after it is peeled and sliced or grated, something to keep in mind when buying for a recipe.

Pumpkin, Squash, and Sage Soup

Pumpkin and butternut squash have similar flavors,
so feel free to adjust the amount of each in this recipe.

INGREDIENTS | SERVES 8

3 sprigs fresh sage

3 cups chopped, fresh pumpkin, skinned

2 cups chopped butternut squash, skinned

1 small white onion, diced

4 cups Vegetable Broth (see recipe in this chapter)

2 bay leaves

2 teaspoons salt

½ cup unsweetened soymilk

1. Place the sage in a piece of cheesecloth and tie closed.

2. Combine all of the ingredients except for the soymilk in a 6-quart slow cooker. Cover and cook over low heat for 4–6 hours, or until the vegetables are very tender.

3. Remove the sage, add the soymilk, and blend using an immersion blender until very smooth.

PER SERVING | Calories: 44 | Fat: 0 g | Protein: 1 g | Sodium: 599 mg | Fiber: 1 g | Carbohydrates: 10 g | Sugar: 3 g

Cheesecloth

Cheesecloth is a handy kitchen tool that can be used for securing fresh herbs, nuts, beans, or many other ingredients. Using cheesecloth, you are able to incorporate a flavor into a dish without having to add the entire ingredient. It's available at grocery stores, and a few yards can usually be purchased for just a couple of dollars.

Dal

Yellow split peas are most commonly used to make dal, but the green variety will work well, too.

INGREDIENTS | SERVES 6

2 cups dried yellow split peas

8 cups water

2 carrots, peeled and diced

½ onion, diced

2 teaspoons cumin

½ teaspoon turmeric

½ teaspoon coriander

2 teaspoons garam masala

¼ teaspoon salt

1. Combine all of the ingredients in a 6-quart slow cooker. Cover and cook over low heat for 6 hours.

2. Season with salt, to taste, before serving.

PER SERVING | Calories: 56 | Fat: 0 g | Protein: 3 g | Sodium: 128 mg | Fiber: 3 g | Carbohydrates: 10 g | Sugar: 4 g

Rustic Cabbage Soup

This cabbage soup isn't just for dieters! Leave the peels on the potatoes and carrots to enhance the rustic feel.

INGREDIENTS | SERVES 6

2 tablespoons olive oil

1 white onion, sliced

½ head of cabbage, shredded

2 russet potatoes, diced

1 celery stalk, sliced

1 carrot, sliced

2 tomatoes, diced

5 cups Vegetable Broth (see recipe in this chapter)

¼ teaspoon salt

¼ teaspoon pepper

1. Heat the olive oil in a small sauté pan over medium-low heat. Add the onions and sauté until softened, about 5 minutes, then transfer to an 8-quart slow cooker.

2. Add all remaining ingredients to the slow cooker except for salt and pepper. Cover and cook on low heat for 8 hours.

3. Add salt and pepper, to taste, before serving.

PER SERVING | Calories: 145 | Fat: 5 g | Protein: 3 g | Sodium: 131 mg | Fiber: 4 g | Carbohydrates: 24 g | Sugar: 7 g

Fava Bean Soup

Before cooking fava beans you should remove them from their pods.

INGREDIENTS | SERVES 6

1 cup shelled fava beans

1 small onion, diced

2 carrots, peeled and diced

2 Yukon Gold potatoes, peeled and diced

2 cups diced, fresh tomatoes

6 cups Vegetable Broth (see recipe in this chapter)

¼ cup chopped and pitted kalamata olives

½ teaspoon red pepper flakes

¼ cup chopped, fresh flat-leaf parsley

¼ teaspoon salt

1. Place all of the ingredients except parsley and salt in a 6-quart slow cooker. Cover and cook on low heat for 4 hours.

2. Before serving, season with salt, to taste, and garnish with fresh parsley.

PER SERVING | Calories: 177 | Fat: 1 g | Protein: 9 g | Sodium: 127 mg | Fiber: 10 g | Carbohydrates: 36 g | Sugar: 7 g

Flat-Leaf Versus Curly Parsley

There is a debate about which of the most commonly used parsley has more flavor, flat leaf or curly, but there is an undeniable difference in texture. Curly leaf parsley tends to be slightly tougher and maintains a lot of its curl when chopped. Flat-leaf, or Italian, parsley is softer.

Carrot-Coconut Soup

*Although coconut milk is high in fat and should be used sparingly,
it's also a good source of iron for vegans.*

INGREDIENTS | SERVES 4

2 tablespoons olive oil

½ onion, diced

3 cloves garlic, minced

1 pound carrots, peeled and chopped

3 cups Vegetable Broth (see recipe in this chapter)

1 stalk lemongrass, sliced

1 tablespoon soy sauce

1 lime, juiced

1 cup coconut milk

¼ teaspoon salt

¼ cup chopped, fresh basil

Choosing Coconut Milk

Coconut milk varies in thickness and fat content. Some are quite thin, and others are more like cream than milk. Most brands of canned coconut milk are very similar, but you can usually see the percentage of coconut milk to water in the list of ingredients to help you select the level of thickness you are looking for.

1. Heat the olive oil in a sauté pan over medium-low heat. Add the onion and sauté until translucent, or about 5 minutes. Add the garlic and sauté for an additional 30 seconds.

2. Place the cooked onion and garlic, carrots, Vegetable Broth, lemongrass, soy sauce, and lime juice into a 6-quart slow cooker. Cover and cook on low heat for 4–6 hours, or until carrots are very tender.

3. Add the coconut milk, then use an immersion blender or traditional blender and purée the soup until very smooth. Season with salt, to taste, and top with fresh chopped basil.

PER SERVING | Calories: 242 | Fat: 19 g | Protein: 3 g | Sodium: 458 mg | Fiber: 4 g | Carbohydrates: 18 g | Sugar: 8 g

Savory Beet Soup

Shallots have a milder flavor than onions and are a better choice for recipes that have subtle flavors.

INGREDIENTS | SERVES 8

2 tablespoons olive oil

2 cloves garlic, minced

2 shallots, diced

4 beets, peeled and chopped

1 Yukon Gold potato, peeled and chopped

4 cups Vegetable Broth (see recipe in this chapter)

½ teaspoon dried thyme

½ teaspoon black pepper

¼ teaspoon salt

1. Heat the olive oil in a sauté pan over medium-low heat. Add the garlic and shallots and sauté for 2 minutes. Transfer to a 6-quart slow cooker.

2. Add the beets, potato, Vegetable Broth, thyme, and pepper. Cover and cook over low heat for 6 hours, or until beets and potatoes are very tender.

3. Use an immersion blender or traditional blender to purée. Season with salt to taste.

PER SERVING | Calories: 84 | Fat: 3.5 g | Protein: 1.5 g | Sodium: 128 mg | Fiber: 2 g | Carbohydrates: 12.5 g | Sugar: 5 g

Simple Split Pea Soup

Split peas break down during cooking and will leave you with a soup that is slightly creamy. To make your soup very smooth, just blend after removing the bay leaves.

INGREDIENTS | SERVES 8

2 cups dried green split peas

7 cups water

2 carrots, peeled and diced

2 stalks celery, sliced

1 white onion, diced

2 bay leaves

½ teaspoon pepper

1 teaspoon salt

3 dashes vegan Worcestershire sauce

1. Place all ingredients in a 6-quart slow cooker. Cover and cook on low for 8 hours.

2. Remove the bay leaves and stir well before serving.

PER SERVING | Calories: 45 | Fat: 0 | Protein: 2.3 g | Sodium: 344 mg | Fiber: 3 g | Carbohydrates: 9 g | Sugar: 54 g

Vegan Vichyssoise

*Vichyssoise is traditionally served cold (and is made using cream, too),
but this warm vegan version will leave you satisfied on a cold day.*

INGREDIENTS | SERVES 6

2 tablespoons Earth Balance Original Buttery Spread

3 leeks (white part only), sliced

1 white onion, sliced

3 Idaho potatoes, peeled and diced

4 cups Vegetable Broth (see recipe in this chapter)

1 bay leaf

½ teaspoon pepper

¼ teaspoon dried thyme

1 cup unsweetened soymilk

¼ teaspoon salt

2 tablespoons chopped chives

Earth Balance

Earth Balance Original Buttery Spread is a popular brand of vegan buttery spread that has a delicious flavor and acts similarly to butter in cooking. Many types of margarine don't melt easily or have a rubbery texture, but Earth Balance Original is very creamy and can be used in all types of recipes.

1. Melt the Earth Balance in a large pan over medium heat. Add the leeks and onions and sauté for 10 minutes. Transfer to a 6-quart slow cooker.

2. Add the potatoes, Vegetable Broth, bay leaf, pepper, and thyme. Cover and cook over low heat for 6 hours. Remove the bay leaf when done.

3. Add the soymilk and purée using an immersion blender or traditional blender.

4. Season with salt to taste, and top with chives before serving.

PER SERVING | Calories: 182 | Fat: 5 g | Protein: 5 g | Sodium: 178 mg | Fiber: 3 g | Carbohydrates: 32 g | Sugar: 6 g

Roasted Red Pepper and Corn Soup

You can roast your own bell peppers for this recipe or use jarred peppers to save a little time.

INGREDIENTS | SERVES 6

6 red bell peppers, halved and seeded

1 cup corn kernels

1 russett potato, peeled and chopped

½ white onion, diced

2 cloves garlic, minced

6 cups Vegetable Broth (see recipe in this chapter)

2 tablespoons white wine vinegar

2 bay leaves

¼ teaspoon pepper

1 teaspoon salt

2 tablespoons chopped cilantro

1. Preheat your oven's broiler.

2. Place the bell peppers on a baking sheet, skin side up, and broil for 15 minutes or until black spots appear. Remove and place the peppers in a paper or plastic bag. Close the bag and let sit for 5 minutes to loosen the skins. Remove the peppers, peel off the skin, and chop.

3. Place the peppers and all remaining ingredients, except cilantro, in a 6-quart slow cooker. Cover and cook over low heat for 6 hours. Remove bay leaves when done.

4. Purée using an immersion blender or traditional blender. Add the cilantro before serving.

PER SERVING | Calories: 106 | Fat: 1 g | Protein: 3 g | Sodium: 402 mg | Fiber: 4 g | Carbohydrates: 23 g | Sugar: 9 g

Creamy Broccoli Soup

Broccoli is loaded with vitamins A and C, making it a must-have veggie in your kitchen.

INGREDIENTS | SERVES 6

6 cups broccoli florets

2 medium russet potatoes, peeled and diced

½ onion, chopped

4 cups Vegetable Broth (see recipe in this chapter)

2 tablespoons Earth Balance Original Buttery Spread

2 tablespoons flour

1 cup unsweetened soymilk

¼ teaspoon salt

In Season

Broccoli fares better during cooler months than it does during hot summer days. Depending on where you live, broccoli is typically at its best during the fall and winter.

1. Place the broccoli, potatoes, onion, and Vegetable Broth in a 6-quart slow cooker. Cover and cook over low heat for 6–8 hours, or until the potatoes are very tender.

2. Use an immersion blender or traditional blender to purée the soup until smooth.

3. Heat the Earth Balance in a small saucepan over low heat. Once melted, add the flour and stir to form a roux. Slowly add the soymilk and whisk until smooth.

4. Add the milk mixture to the soup, stir until well combined, and season with salt to taste.

PER SERVING | Calories: 156 | Fat: 5 g | Protein: 5 g | Sodium: 197 mg | Fiber: 4.5 g | Carbohydrates: 24 g | Sugar: 6 g

CHAPTER 4

Stews

Brunswick Stew

Try adding barbeque sauce to this stew to spice things up.

INGREDIENTS | SERVES 4

4 cups Vegetable Broth (see Chapter 3)

1 (15-ounce) can diced tomatoes

1 (6-ounce) can tomato paste

1 cup sliced okra

1 cup corn

1 cup frozen lima beans

2 cups diced seitan

¼ teaspoon dried rosemary

¼ teaspoon dried oregano

2 teaspoons vegan Worcestershire sauce

⅛ teaspoon salt

⅛ teaspoon pepper

In a 4-quart slow cooker, add all ingredients. Cover and cook on low heat for 5–6 hours.

PER SERVING | Calories: 273 | Fat: 6 g | Protein: 15 g | Sodium: 636 mg | Fiber: 7 g | Carbohydrates: 44 g | Sugar: 10 g

Debate on Origin

Some claim that Brunswick stew was first served in Brunswick, Georgia, in 1898, while others say it was created in Brunswick County, Virginia, in 1828. Today, Brunswick stew recipe ingredients vary by region.

Jamaican Red Bean Stew

*Make your own jerk seasoning by combining thyme, allspice, black pepper,
cinnamon, cayenne, onion powder, and nutmeg.*

INGREDIENTS | SERVES 4

2 tablespoons olive oil

½ onion, diced

2 garlic cloves, minced

1 (15-ounce) can diced tomatoes

3 cups diced sweet potatoes, peeled

2 (15-ounce) cans red kidney beans, drained

1 cup coconut milk

3 cups Vegetable Broth (see Chapter 3)

2 teaspoons jerk seasoning

2 teaspoons curry powder

⅛ teaspoon salt

⅛ teaspoon pepper

1. In a sauté pan over medium heat, add the olive oil, then sauté the onion and garlic for about 3 minutes.

2. In a 4-quart slow cooker, add all ingredients. Cover and cook on low heat for 6 hours.

PER SERVING | Calories: 493 | Fat: 19 g | Protein: 15 g | Sodium: 755 mg | Fiber: 15 g | Carbohydrates: 60 g | Sugar: 11 g

Super Greens Stew

*Kale and Swiss chard can hold up during long cooking times,
but a more delicate green, such as spinach, would break down more.*

INGREDIENTS | SERVES 6

2 cups chopped kale

2 cups chopped Swiss chard

1 (15-ounce) can chickpeas, drained

¼ onion, diced

1 carrot, peeled and sliced

2 cloves garlic, minced

6 cups Vegetable Broth (see Chapter 3)

1½ teaspoons salt

½ teaspoon pepper

1 sprig rosemary

½ teaspoon dried marjoram

In a 4-quart slow cooker, add all ingredients. Cover and cook on low heat for 6 hours.

PER SERVING | Calories: 128 | Fat: 1.4 g | Protein: 6 g | Sodium: 638 mg | Fiber: 5 g | Carbohydrates: 20 g | Sugar: 2 g

Mediterranean Vegetable Stew

Try serving this stew with large pieces of warm pita bread and a scoop of hummus.

INGREDIENTS | SERVES 6

2 tablespoons extra-virgin olive oil

4 garlic cloves, chopped

1 red onion, chopped

1 red bell pepper, seeded and chopped

1 eggplant, chopped

1 (15-ounce) can artichokes, drained and chopped

⅓ cup chopped and pitted kalamata olives

2 (15-ounce) cans diced tomatoes

4 cups Vegetable Broth (see Chapter 3)

1 teaspoon red pepper flakes

½ teaspoon dried oregano

½ teaspoon dried parsley

1 teaspoon salt

½ teaspoon pepper

In a 4-quart slow cooker, add all ingredients. Cover and cook on low heat for 4–6 hours.

PER SERVING | Calories: 214 | Fat: 6 g | Protein: 6 g | Sodium: 522 mg | Fiber: 8 g | Carbohydrates: 31 g | Sugar: 12 g

Preparing Eggplant

Some people salt eggplant prior to cooking in order to remove bitterness, but this step is not required for making delicious eggplant dishes. The skins can be removed, but this also is not necessary. Eggplant, called aubergine in almost all other parts of the world, can be boiled, steamed, sautéed, stir-fried, deep-fried, braised, baked, grilled, broiled, and microwaved.

Curried Seitan Stew

Adding a small amount of soy sauce to a curry dish gives it a richness that is normally achieved with fish sauce in recipes that aren't vegan.

INGREDIENTS | SERVES 4

2 tablespoons olive oil

½ onion, chopped

2 cloves garlic, minced

1 teaspoon minced, fresh ginger

2 tablespoons Panang curry paste

1 teaspoon paprika

1 teaspoon sugar

½ teaspoon cayenne pepper

1 teaspoon soy sauce

1 (14-ounce) can coconut milk

3 cups Vegetable Broth (see Chapter 3)

2 cups cubed seitan

½ teaspoon salt

¼ teaspoon pepper

¼ cup chopped cilantro

1. In a 4-quart slow cooker, add all ingredients except the cilantro. Cover and cook on low heat for 4 hours.

2. Garnish with cilantro before serving.

PER SERVING | Calories: 322 | Fat: 28 g | Protein: 6.5 g | Sodium: 426 mg | Fiber: 6 g | Carbohydrates: 16 g | Sugar: 6 g

Étouffée

Vegan shrimp can be purchased online at VeganStore.com (www.veganstore.com).

INGREDIENTS | SERVES 6

½ cup Earth Balance Original Buttery Spread

1 onion, diced

3 celery ribs, chopped

1 carrot, diced

3 cloves garlic, minced

1 green bell pepper, chopped

¼ cup flour

1 cup water

2 teaspoons Cajun seasoning

1 (8.8-ounce) package vegan shrimp

1 lemon, juiced

½ teaspoon salt

¼ teaspoon black pepper

4 cups cooked white rice

½ cup chopped parsley

Cajun Seasoning

To make your own Cajun seasoning, use a blend of equal parts cayenne pepper, black pepper, paprika, garlic powder, onion powder, salt, and thyme.

1. In a sauté pan over medium heat, melt the Earth Balance. Sauté the onion, celery, carrot, garlic, and green bell pepper until soft, about 5–7 minutes. Stir in the flour to make a roux.

2. Add the roux to a 4-quart slow cooker. Whisk in the water, Cajun seasoning, vegan shrimp, lemon juice, salt, and pepper. Cover and cook on low heat for 4–5 hours.

3. Serve over the white rice and garnish with parsley.

PER SERVING | Calories: 410 | Fat: 167 g | Protein: 15 g | Sodium: 381 mg | Fiber: 4 g | Carbohydrates: 49 g | Sugar: 4 g

Posole

This rich-tasting stew just needs a sprinkling of shredded red cabbage to make it perfect.

INGREDIENTS | SERVES 6

8 large dried New Mexican red chilies

1½ quarts Vegetable Broth (see Chapter 3)

3 cloves garlic, minced

2 tablespoons lime juice

1 tablespoon ground cumin

1 tablespoon oregano

1 (7-ounce) package Gardein Chick'n Strips

¾ cup flour

1 teaspoon canola oil

1 large onion, sliced

40 ounces canned hominy

Citrus Leftovers

If you have a small amount of juice left from a lemon or lime, pour it into an ice cube tray freezer, one well at a time, and freeze. Leftover zest can also be saved. Place the zest in a freezer bag and refrigerate for up to 1 week or freeze in a freezer-safe container for up to 1 month.

1. Seed the chilies, reserving the seeds.

2. In a dry, hot frying pan, heat the chilies until warmed through and fragrant, about 2–3 minutes. Do not burn or brown them.

3. In a medium pot, place the chilies and seeds, 1 quart broth, garlic, lime juice, cumin, and oregano. Bring to a boil and continue to boil for 20 minutes.

4. Meanwhile, in a plastic bag, toss the Chick'n Strips with the flour to coat. Heat the oil in a large nonstick skillet and brown the vegan meat on all sides, about 3 minutes.

5. Add the onions and cook about 5 minutes, or until the onions are soft.

6. In a 4-quart slow cooker, pour in the unused broth, hominy, the onion, and Chick'n Strips mixture.

7. Strain the chile-stock mixture through a mesh sieve, and pour into the slow cooker insert, mashing down with a wooden spoon to press out the pulp and juice. Discard the seeds and remaining solids. Cook on low for 8 hours.

PER SERVING | Calories: 824 | Fat: 4 g | Protein: 22.5 g | Sodium: 147.5 mg | Fiber: 11 g | Carbohydrates: 182 g | Sugar: 12 g

White Bean Cassoulet

The longer you cook this cassoulet, the creamier it will get as the cannellini beans break down.

INGREDIENTS | SERVES 8

1 pound dried cannellini beans

2 cups boiling water

1 ounce dried porcini mushrooms

2 leeks, sliced

1 teaspoon canola oil

2 parsnips, diced

2 carrots, diced

2 stalks celery, diced

½ teaspoon ground fennel

1 teaspoon crushed rosemary

1 teaspoon dried chervil

⅛ teaspoon cloves

¼ teaspoon salt

¼ teaspoon freshly ground black pepper

2 cups Vegetable Broth (see Chapter 3)

1. The night before making the soup, place the beans in a 4-quart slow cooker. Fill with water to 1 inch below the top of the insert. Soak overnight.

2. Drain the beans and return them to the slow cooker.

3. In a heat-proof bowl, pour the boiling water over the dried mushrooms and soak for 15 minutes.

4. Slice only the white and light green parts of the leek into ¼-inch rounds. Cut the rounds in half.

   In a nonstick skillet, heat the oil. Add the parsnip, carrots, celery, and leeks. Sauté for 1 minute, just until the color of the vegetables brightens. Add to the slow cooker along with the remaining spices.

5. Add the mushrooms, their soaking liquid, and the broth, and stir. Cook on low for 8–10 hours.

PER SERVING | Calories: 220 | Fat: 1.5 g | Protein: 15 g | Sodium: 170 mg | Fiber: 10 g | Carbohydrates: 39 g | Sugar: 6 g

Korean-Style Hot Pot

Serve this hot and spicy main dish with sides of steamed rice and kimchi (a Korean condiment of fermented vegetables).

INGREDIENTS | SERVES 8

3 bunches baby bok choy
8 cups water
8 ounces sliced crimini mushrooms
12 ounces extra-firm tofu, cubed
3 cloves garlic, thinly sliced
¼ teaspoon sesame oil
1 tablespoon crushed red pepper flakes
7 ounces enoki mushrooms

1. Remove the leaves of the baby bok choy. Wash thoroughly.

2. Place the whole leaves in a 4-quart slow cooker. Add the water, crimini mushrooms, tofu, garlic, sesame oil, and crushed red pepper. Stir.

3. Cook on low for 8 hours.

4. Add the enoki mushrooms and stir. Cook an additional 30 minutes.

PER SERVING | Calories: 80 | Fat: 2 g | Protein: 9 g | Sodium: 230 mg | Fiber: 4 g | Carbohydrates: 11 g | Sugar: 3 g

Succotash Stew

Try adding chopped okra to this versatile Southern stew.

INGREDIENTS | SERVES 6

1 pound dry lima beans
8 cups water, divided
2 (14-ounce) cans corn, drained
2 (14-ounce) cans diced tomatoes
2 bay leaves
1 teaspoon dried thyme
1 teaspoon dried oregano
¼ teaspoon cayenne pepper
¼ teaspoon salt
⅛ teaspoon black pepper

1. Place the dry lima beans and 7 cups water in a 4-quart slow cooker, cover, and cook on high heat for 4 hours. Drain the lima beans.

2. Place the drained lima beans, 1 cup water, corn, tomatoes, bay leaves, thyme, oregano, cayenne pepper, salt, and black pepper in the slow cooker and cook on low heat for 4 hours.

PER SERVING | Calories: 381 | Fat: 2 g | Protein: 20 g | Sodium: 730 mg | Fiber: 18 g | Carbohydrates: 77 g | Sugar: 12 g

Seitan Bourguignon

Better Than Bouillon's No Beef Base is a good vegan alternative to beef stock.

INGREDIENTS | SERVES 6

2 tablespoons olive oil

1 pound cooked seitan, cut into 2-inch cubes

2 carrots, sliced

1 onion, sliced

1 teaspoon salt

2 tablespoons flour

2 cups red wine

2 cups vegan beef stock

1 tablespoon tomato paste

2 cloves garlic, minced

½ teaspoon dried thyme

1 bay leaf

¼ teaspoon pepper

1 tablespoon Earth Balance Original Buttery Spread

18 whole pearl onions, peeled

2 cups sliced button mushrooms

1. Heat the olive oil in a sauté pan over medium heat. Sauté the seitan, carrots, and onion until soft, about 7 minutes. Stir in the salt and flour.

2. In a 4-quart slow cooker, add the seitan mixture. Whisk in the red wine and vegan beef broth, then add all remaining ingredients.

3. Cover and cook over low heat for 6–8 hours.

PER SERVING | Calories: 280 | Fat: 8 g | Protein: 20 g | Sodium: 805 mg | Fiber: 3 g | Carbohydrates: 15 g | Sugar: 3.5 g

Seitan

Seitan is made from wheat gluten and is often used as a vegetarian substitute for all types of meat. It's one of the easiest meat substitutes to cook with at home.

Chunky Mushroom Trio

All of the delicious mushrooms in this recipe create a very thick and chunky stew.
You can eat it plain or served over a bed of steamed white rice.

INGREDIENTS | SERVES 6

2 tablespoons olive oil

1 onion, chopped

1 pound white button mushrooms, chopped

1 pound shiitake mushrooms, stemmed and chopped

1 pound oyster mushrooms, stemmed and chopped

3 cloves garlic, minced

½ pound red potatoes, chopped into bite-sized pieces

4 cups Vegetable Broth (see Chapter 3)

1 tablespoon soy sauce

½ cup red wine (optional)

1 teaspoon dried thyme

¼ teaspoon salt

⅛ teaspoon black pepper

1. Add the olive oil to the slow cooker and sauté the onion and mushrooms on medium-high heat for 3–5 minutes. Add the garlic and sauté for 1 minute more.

2. Add the rest of the ingredients and cook on medium-high heat for 3–4 hours.

PER SERVING | Calories: 109 | Fat: 5 g | Protein: 4 g | Sodium: 264 mg | Fiber: 3 g | Carbohydrates: 15 g | Sugar: 3 g

Cooking with Alcohol

In recipes like this one, which contain a significant amount of alcohol, you shouldn't expect all of the alcohol to "cook off." If you are pregnant, cooking for a child, or just like to avoid alcohol, you may want to skip this recipe.

Potato and Lentil Stew

If you prefer a creamier stew, try using red lentils instead of green.
They break down much faster.

INGREDIENTS | SERVES 6

2 tablespoons olive oil

1 onion, diced

2 carrots, sliced

2 stalks celery, chopped

3 cloves garlic, minced

½ pound potatoes, chopped into bite-size pieces

1 pound dried green lentils

4 cups water

4 cups Vegetable Broth (see Chapter 3)

1 tablespoon soy sauce

1 bay leaf

½ teaspoon salt

⅛ teaspoon black pepper

1. Add the olive oil to a 4-quart slow cooker and sauté the onion, carrot, and celery on medium-high heat for 3–5 minutes. Add the garlic and sauté for 1 minute more.

2. Add the rest of the ingredients and cook on low heat for 6 hours.

PER SERVING | Calories: 360 | Fat: 5 g | Protein: 20 g | Sodium: 385 mg | Fiber: 24 g | Carbohydrates: 57 g | Sugar: 5 g

Hoppin' John Stew

In the South, eating Hoppin' John on New Year's Day is a tradition and thought to bring good luck throughout the year.

INGREDIENTS | SERVES 6

2 tablespoons olive oil
1 onion, diced
2 stalks celery, chopped
3 cloves garlic, minced
1 pound dried black-eyed peas
3 cups water
4 cups Vegetable Broth (see Chapter 3)
1 tablespoon soy sauce
1 bay leaf
1 teaspoon hot sauce
½ teaspoon salt
⅛ teaspoon black pepper
6 cups cooked white rice

1. Add the olive oil to a 4-quart slow cooker and sauté the onion and celery on medium-high heat for 3–5 minutes. Add the garlic and sauté for 1 minute more.

2. Add the rest of the ingredients, except for the rice, and cook on high heat for 5–6 hours.

3. Serve the stew over the cooked white rice in a bowl.

PER SERVING | Calories: 553 | Fat: 6 g | Protein: 22 g | Sodium: 195 mg | Fiber: 9 g | Carbohydrates: 104 g | Sugar: 7.5 g

Dried Versus Canned Beans

You can use dried or canned beans in almost any recipe that calls for one or the other. The difference is the cost, cooking time, and health benefits of each. To use canned beans instead of dried in this recipe, reduce the heat to low and cook the soup for only 2 hours.

Fall Pumpkin Stew

Have some festive fun by serving this soup in small, hollowed-out pumpkins.

INGREDIENTS | SERVES 6

3 tablespoons Earth Balance Original Buttery Spread

1 onion, diced

2 carrots, sliced

2 stalks celery, chopped

3 cloves garlic, minced

1 pumpkin, rind and seeds removed, flesh cut into ½-inch chunks

2 sweet potatoes, cut into bite-sized pieces

1 (14-ounce) can diced tomatoes

4 cups Vegetable Broth (see Chapter 3)

1 tablespoon soy sauce

1 bay leaf

1 teaspoon dried thyme

¼ teaspoon salt

1. Add the Earth Balance to a 4-quart slow cooker and sauté the onion, carrot, and celery on medium-high heat for 3–5 minutes. Add the garlic and sauté for 1 minute more.

2. Add the rest of the ingredients and cook on low heat 6 hours.

PER SERVING | Calories: 135 | Fat: 6 g | Protein: 2.5 g | Sodium: 460 mg | Fiber: 3.5 g | Carbohydrates: 20 g | Sugar: 7 g

Wild Mushroom Ragout

For a more refined flavor, try substituting the onion with shallots in this recipe.

INGREDIENTS | SERVES 4

2 tablespoons olive oil

1 onion, diced

½ pound white button mushrooms, sliced

½ pound shiitake mushrooms, sliced

½ pound oyster mushrooms, sliced

3 cloves garlic, minced

¼ teaspoon salt

⅛ teaspoon black pepper

1 tablespoon chopped rosemary

1 tablespoon chopped sage

2 cups diced tomatoes

2 cups Vegetable Broth (see Chapter 3)

1. Add the olive oil to a 4-quart slow cooker and sauté the onion and mushrooms on medium-high heat for 4–5 minutes. Add the garlic, salt, and black pepper and sauté for 1 minute more.

2. Add the rosemary, sage, tomatoes, and Vegetable Broth and cook over low heat for 2 hours.

PER SERVING | Calories: 148 | Fat: 7 g | Protein: 2 g | Sodium: 171 mg | Fiber: 2 g | Carbohydrates: 10 g | Sugar: 3 g

Mushroom Varieties

Button mushrooms are a milder type of mushroom with little flavor, but they are inexpensive and can be used in combination with more flavorful varieties. Shiitake, oyster, chanterelle, and hen of the woods are more expensive varieties that have wonderful texture and flavor.

White Bean Ragout

Ragout is another word for stew. It can be made with any combination of vegetables, herbs, and liquids.

INGREDIENTS | SERVES 4

2 tablespoons olive oil

1 onion, diced

5 cloves garlic, minced

2 (14-ounce) cans navy beans, drained

1 (14-ounce) can diced tomatoes

3 cups water

¼ cup tomato paste

½ cup chopped, fresh parsley

2 tablespoons chopped, fresh sage

¼ teaspoon salt

⅛ teaspoon black pepper

1. Add the olive oil to a 4-quart slow cooker and sauté the onion on medium-high heat for 3–5 minutes. Add the garlic and sauté for 1 minute more.

2. Add the navy beans, tomatoes, water, tomato paste, parsley, sage, salt, and black pepper, and cook on low heat for 4 hours.

PER SERVING | Calories: 790 | Fat: 8 g | Protein: 45 g | Sodium: 333 mg | Fiber: 41 g | Carbohydrates: 139 g | Sugar: 25 g

New England Corn Chowder

This chowder is even better with fresh corn, when it is in season. Just remove the kernels from the husk and use the same amount of corn.

INGREDIENTS | SERVES 4

½ cup Earth Balance Original Buttery Spread

1 onion, diced

3 cloves garlic, minced

¼ cup flour

4 cups unsweetened soymilk

3 potatoes, peeled and diced

2 cups frozen corn

2 cups Vegetable Broth (see Chapter 3)

½ teaspoon dried thyme

½ teaspoon salt

1. Add the Earth Balance to a 4-quart slow cooker and sauté the onion on medium heat for 4–5 minutes. Add the garlic and sauté for 1 minute more.

2. Slowly stir in the flour with a whisk and create a roux. Stir in the soymilk and continue whisking until very smooth.

3. Add the remaining ingredients and cook on low heat for 3–4 hours.

PER SERVING | Calories: 565 | Fat: 27 g | Protein: 14 g | Sodium: 698 mg | Fiber: 8 g | Carbohydrates: 68 g | Sugar: 14 g

Gumbo Z'Herbes

You won't miss the meat with all the delicious flavors in this gumbo. As they say in New Orleans, "laissez les bons temps rouler!" Or "let the good times roll!"

INGREDIENTS | SERVES 6

½ cup olive oil
1 onion, chopped
1 green bell pepper, chopped
2 stalks celery, chopped
4 cloves garlic, minced
½ cup flour
4 cups Vegetable Broth (see Chapter 3)
2 cups chopped okra
½ teaspoon dried thyme
½ teaspoon dried oregano
1 teaspoon salt
½ teaspoon black pepper
¼ teaspoon red pepper flakes
6 cups cooked white rice

1. Add the olive oil to a 4-quart slow cooker and sauté the onion, bell pepper, and celery on medium heat for 4–5 minutes. Add the garlic and sauté for 1 minute more.

2. Slowly stir in the flour with a whisk and create a roux. Pour in the Vegetable Broth and continue to whisk to remove all lumps.

3. Add the rest of the ingredients, except rice, and cook on medium-high heat for 3–4 hours. Serve over the cooked white rice.

PER SERVING | Calories: 474 | Fat: 18 g | Protein: 7 g | Sodium: 408 mg | Fiber: 3 g | Carbohydrates: 69 g | Sugar: 3 g

The Holy Trinity

The base of some of New Orleans's most well-known dishes is referred to as the "holy trinity." It contains equal parts onion, bell pepper, and celery.

Sweet Potato and Cranberry Stew

You can call it "Thanksgiving in a bowl," because this spiced stew is loaded with holiday flavors such as sweet potato, cranberry, cinnamon, and nutmeg.

INGREDIENTS | SERVES 6

2 tablespoons olive oil

1 onion, chopped

3 garlic cloves, minced

2 teaspoons turmeric

1 teaspoon curry powder

1 teaspoon cumin

1 teaspoon cinnamon

¼ teaspoon nutmeg

4 sweet potatoes, peeled and cut into bite-sized cubes

2 cups frozen cranberries

6 cups Vegetable Broth (see Chapter 3)

½ teaspoon salt

⅛ teaspoon black pepper

1. Add the olive oil to a 4-quart slow cooker and sauté the onion on medium heat for 4–5 minutes. Add the garlic and sauté for 1 minute more.

2. Add the rest of the ingredients and cook on low heat for 6 hours.

PER SERVING | Calories: 154 | Fat: 5 g | Protein: 2 g | Sodium: 246 mg | Fiber: 5 g | Carbohydrates: 27 g | Sugar: 8 g

CHAPTER 5

Chili

Southwest Vegetable Chili

Southwest cuisine is similar to Mexican food and includes a wide variety of peppers, such as the jalapeños, bell peppers, chipotle (smoked jalapeño), and chili powder, found in this recipe.

INGREDIENTS | SERVES 4

1 (28-ounce) can diced tomatoes

1 (15-ounce) can red kidney beans

1 onion, chopped

1 green bell pepper, chopped

1 red bell pepper, chopped

1 medium zucchini, chopped

1 squash, chopped

¼ cup chopped pickled jalapeños

2 tablespoons chili powder

2 tablespoons garlic powder

2 tablespoons cumin

1 teaspoon chipotle powder

⅛ teaspoon dried thyme

¼ teaspoon black pepper

Add all ingredients to a 4-quart slow cooker. Cover and cook on low heat for 5 hours.

PER SERVING | Calories: 206 | Fat: 3 g | Protein: 11 g | Sodium: 340 mg | Fiber: 13 g | Carbohydrates: 40 g | Sugar: 13 g

Cincinnati Chili

Cincinnati chili is native to the state of Ohio and typically is flavored with cinnamon and eaten over spaghetti or on hot dogs.

INGREDIENTS | SERVES 4

1 onion, chopped

1 (12-ounce) package frozen veggie burger crumbles

3 cloves garlic, minced

1 cup tomato sauce

1 cup water

2 tablespoons red wine vinegar

2 tablespoons chili powder

½ teaspoon cumin

½ teaspoon ground cinnamon

½ teaspoon paprika

½ teaspoon ground allspice

1 tablespoon light brown sugar

1 tablespoon unsweetened cocoa powder

1 teaspoon hot pepper sauce

16 ounces cooked spaghetti

¼ cup vegan cheddar cheese (optional)

¼ cup onion, diced (optional)

¼ cup cooked pinto beans (optional)

1. In a 4-quart slow cooker, add all ingredients except for the spaghetti and optional ingredients. Cover and cook on low heat for 5 hours.

2. Serve the chili over the spaghetti and top with (optional) vegan cheese, onions, and pinto beans.

PER SERVING | Calories: 329 | Fat: 6 g | Protein: 24.5 g | Sodium: 783 mg | Fiber: 2 g | Carbohydrates: 50 g | Sugar: 8 g

Ways to Serve

Cincinnati chili is known for being served up to five ways: Two-way means chili and spaghetti; three-way means chili, spaghetti, and cheddar cheese; four-way means chili, spaghetti, vegan cheese, and onions; and five-way means chili, spaghetti, cheese, onions, and pinto beans!

Chili con "Carne"

Try Boca Ground Crumbles in this fast recipe as a vegan alternative to ground beef.

INGREDIENTS | SERVES 4

½ cup diced onion

½ cup diced bell pepper

1 (12-ounce) package frozen veggie burger crumbles

2 cloves garlic, minced

1 (15-ounce) can kidney beans, rinsed and drained

2 cups Vegetable Broth (see Chapter 3)

1 tablespoon chili powder

½ tablespoon chipotle powder

½ tablespoon cumin

1 teaspoon thyme

1 tablespoon oregano

2 cups diced, fresh tomatoes

1 tablespoon tomato paste

1 tablespoon cider vinegar

1 teaspoon salt

Add all ingredients to a 4-quart slow cooker. Cover and cook on low heat for 5 hours.

PER SERVING | Calories: 194 | Fat: 3.5 g | Protein: 13 g | Sodium: 959 mg | Fiber: 9 g | Carbohydrates: 29 g | Sugar: 8 g

Vegan Beef

In addition to Boca Ground Crumbles, there are other types of vegan ground beef on the market. Try Gimme Lean Ground Beef Style, Match Ground Beef, or dehydrated textured vegetable protein (TVP).

Shredded "Chicken" Chili

*There are many vegan chicken substitutes on the market,
but you can also use shredded seitan to replace the meat.*

INGREDIENTS | SERVES 4

½ cup diced onion

½ cup diced bell pepper

1 (7-ounce) package Gardein Chick'n Strips, shredded by hand

2 cloves garlic, minced

1 (15-ounce) can kidney beans, rinsed and drained

2 cups Vegetable Broth (see Chapter 3)

1 tablespoon chili powder

½ tablespoon chipotle powder

½ tablespoon cumin

1 teaspoon thyme

1 tablespoon oregano

1 (15-ounce) can diced tomatoes, drained

1 tablespoon tomato paste

1 tablespoon cider vinegar

1 teaspoon salt

Add all ingredients to a 4-quart slow cooker. Cover and cook on low heat for 5 hours.

PER SERVING | Calories: 219 | Fat: 4.5 g | Protein: 16 g | Sodium: 383 mg | Fiber: 9 g | Carbohydrates: 31 g | Sugar: 9 g

Five-Pepper Chili

Sound the alarm! This chili will set mouths aflame.

INGREDIENTS | SERVES 8

1 onion, diced

1 jalapeño, seeded and minced

1 habanero pepper, seeded and minced

1 bell pepper, diced

1 poblano pepper, seeded and diced

2 cloves garlic, minced

2 (15-ounce) cans crushed tomatoes

2 cups diced, fresh tomatoes

2 tablespoons chili powder

1 tablespoon cumin

½ tablespoon cayenne pepper

2 tablespoons vegan Worcestershire sauce

2 (15-ounce) cans pinto beans

1 teaspoon salt

¼ teaspoon black pepper

Add all ingredients to a 4-quart slow cooker. Cover and cook on low heat for 5 hours.

PER SERVING | Calories: 142 | Fat: 2 g | Protein: 7 g | Sodium: 820 mg | Fiber: 8 g | Carbohydrates: 27 g | Sugar: 6 g

Hot, Hot, Hot

Since peppers vary greatly in regard to how hot they are, the Scoville scale was designed to measure this heat. Here are the peppers in this recipe, from mildest to hottest: poblano, jalapeño, habanero.

Red Bean Chili

In the United States, "red beans" most commonly refers to kidney beans.

INGREDIENTS | SERVES 4

2 (15-ounce) cans red kidney beans, drained

½ cup diced onion

2 cloves garlic, minced

2 cups Vegetable Broth (see Chapter 3)

1 tablespoon chili powder

½ tablespoon chipotle powder

½ tablespoon cumin

½ tablespoon paprika

1 (15-ounce) can tomatoes, diced

½ teaspoon salt

¼ teaspoon black pepper

Add all ingredients to a 4-quart slow cooker. Cover and cook on low heat for 5 hours.

PER SERVING | Calories: 221 | Fat: 1.5 g | Protein: 12 g | Sodium: 1, 008 mg | Fiber: 14 g | Carbohydrates: 42 g | Sugar: 8.5 g

Three-Bean Chili

*Using dried beans will save you a little money on this recipe,
but be sure to soak the beans overnight to save some cooking time.*

INGREDIENTS | SERVES 8

1 (15-ounce) can pinto beans, drained

1 (15-ounce) can black beans, drained

1 (15-ounce) can Great Northern white beans, drained

1 onion, diced

3 cloves garlic, minced

3 cups Vegetable Broth (see Chapter 3)

1 tablespoon chili powder

½ tablespoon chipotle powder

½ tablespoon cumin

½ tablespoon paprika

1 (15-ounce) can diced tomatoes

¼ teaspoon black pepper

Add all ingredients to a 4-quart slow cooker. Cover and cook on low heat for 5 hours.

PER SERVING | Calories: 293 | Fat: 1.5 g | Protein: 17 g | Sodium: 332 mg | Fiber: 16.5 g | Carbohydrates: 54 g | Sugar: 8 g

Sweet Potato Chili

Sweet potatoes are great sources of fiber and beta carotene,
making this chili healthy and delicious.

INGREDIENTS | SERVES 4

1 red onion, diced

1 jalapeño, seeded and minced

3 cloves garlic, minced

1 (15-ounce) can black beans, drained

1 sweet potato, peeled and diced

3 tablespoons chili powder

1 tablespoon paprika

1 teaspoon dried oregano

1 teaspoon ground cumin

½ teaspoon chipotle powder

1 (28-ounce) can diced tomatoes, drained

2 cups Vegetable Broth (see Chapter 3)

¼ teaspoon black pepper

1 lime, juiced

¼ cup chopped cilantro

1. In a 4-quart slow cooker, add all ingredients except the lime and cilantro. Cover and cook on low heat for 8 hours.

2. When the chili is done cooking, mix in the lime juice and garnish with the cilantro.

PER SERVING | Calories: 201 | Fat: 2 g | Protein: 9 g | Sodium: 669 mg | Fiber: 12 g | Carbohydrates: 40 g | Sugar: 11 g

What Is Chili Powder?

Chili powder is made from grinding dried chilies, and may be created from a blend of different types of chilies or just one variety. The most commonly used chilies are red peppers and cayenne peppers.

Fajita Chili

Recreate the flavor of sizzling restaurant fajitas in your own home!

INGREDIENTS | SERVES 6

1 red onion, diced

1 jalapeño, seeded and minced

3 cloves garlic, minced

1 (15-ounce) can black beans, drained

1 (15-ounce) can diced tomatoes, drained

1 (7-ounce) package Gardein Chick'n Strips, cut into bite-sized pieces

2 cups Vegetable Broth (see Chapter 3)

2 teaspoons chili powder

1 teaspoon sugar

1 teaspoon paprika

¼ teaspoon garlic powder

¼ teaspoon cayenne pepper

¼ teaspoon cumin

1 teaspoon salt

¼ teaspoon black pepper

Add all ingredients to a 4-quart slow cooker. Cover and cook on low heat for 5 hours.

PER SERVING | Calories: 170 | Fat: 3.5 g | Protein: 14 g | Sodium: 727 mg | Fiber: 5 g | Carbohydrates: 19 g | Sugar: 3 g

Simplify This Recipe

One way to simplify this recipe is to use a packet of fajita seasoning (sold in the international aisle in many stores) in place of the chili powder, sugar, paprika, garlic powder, cayenne pepper, cumin, salt, and black pepper.

Acorn Squash Chili

Acorn squash keeps its shape in this chili, giving it a chunky texture.

INGREDIENTS | SERVES 8

2 cups cubed acorn squash

30 ounces canned petite diced tomatoes

2 stalks celery, diced

1 medium onion, diced

3 cloves garlic, minced

2 carrots, diced

1 teaspoon mesquite liquid smoke

2 teaspoons hot sauce

1 teaspoon chili powder

1 teaspoon paprika

1 teaspoon oregano

1 teaspoon smoked paprika

1 (15-ounce) can kidney beans, drained and rinsed

1 (15-ounce) can cannellini beans, drained and rinsed

1 cup fresh corn kernels

1. In a 4-quart slow cooker, add all ingredients except the corn. Cover and cook for 8 hours on low.

2. Add the corn and stir. Cover and continue to cook on low for 30 minutes. Stir before serving.

PER SERVING | Calories: 170 | Fat: 1.5 g | Protein: 8 g | Sodium: 417 mg | Fiber: 9 g | Carbohydrates: 32 g | Sugar: 6 g

Summer Chili

This chili is full of summer vegetables, and you can add vegan chicken for a heartier dish.

INGREDIENTS | SERVES 8

1 bulb fennel, diced

4 radishes, diced

2 stalks celery including leaves, diced

2 carrots, cut into coin-sized pieces

1 medium onion, diced

1 shallot, diced

4 cloves garlic, sliced

1 habanero pepper, diced

1 (15-ounce) can cannellini beans, drained and rinsed

1 (12-ounce) can tomato paste

½ teaspoon dried oregano

½ teaspoon black pepper

½ teaspoon crushed rosemary

½ teaspoon cayenne

½ teaspoon ground chipotle

1 teaspoon chili powder

1 teaspoon tarragon

¼ teaspoon cumin

¼ teaspoon celery seed

2 medium zucchini, cubed

10 Campari tomatoes, quartered

1 cup corn kernels

1. In a 4-quart slow cooker, add the fennel, radishes, celery, carrots, onion, shallot, garlic, habanero, beans, tomato paste, and all spices. Stir and then cook on low for 6–7 hours.

2. Stir in the zucchini, tomatoes, and corn. Cook for an additional 30 minutes on high. Stir before serving.

PER SERVING | Calories: 187 | Fat: 2 g | Protein: 7 g | Sodium: 532 mg | Fiber: 8 g | Carbohydrates: 31 g | Sugar: 10 g

Campari Tomatoes

Campari is a brand of tomatoes that are grown on the vine and have a sweet, juicy taste. They are round and on the small side, but not as small as cherry tomatoes.

Black Bean, Corn, and Fresh Tomato Chili

Tofutti makes a delicious nondairy sour cream called Sour Supreme, which can be found in some national grocery store chains.

INGREDIENTS | SERVES 4

1 red onion, diced

1 jalapeño, seeded and minced

3 cloves garlic, minced

1 (15-ounce) can black beans, drained

1 (15-ounce) can corn, drained

3 tablespoons chili powder

1 tablespoon paprika

1 teaspoon dried oregano

1 teaspoon ground cumin

½ teaspoon chipotle powder

2 cups Vegetable Broth (see Chapter 3)

½ teaspoon salt

¼ teaspoon black pepper

2 diced cups tomato

¼ cup chopped cilantro

4 tablespoons vegan sour cream

1. In a 4-quart slow cooker, add all ingredients except tomatoes, cilantro, and sour cream. Cover and cook on low heat for 5 hours.

2. When the chili is done cooking, mix in the tomatoes and garnish with the cilantro. Top with vegan sour cream.

PER SERVING | Calories: 220 | Fat: 3 g | Protein: 10 g | Sodium: 1,005 mg | Fiber: 11 g | Carbohydrates: 44 g | Sugar: 7 g

Lentil Chili

Before using dried lentils, rinse them well and pick through to remove any debris or undesirable pieces.

INGREDIENTS | SERVES 6

1 cup uncooked lentils

1 onion, diced

3 cloves garlic, minced

4 cups Vegetable Broth (see Chapter 3)

¼ cup tomato paste

1 cup chopped carrots

1 cup chopped celery

1 (15-ounce) can diced tomatoes, drained

2 tablespoons chili powder

½ tablespoon paprika

1 teaspoon dried oregano

1 teaspoon cumin

1 teaspoon salt

¼ teaspoon black pepper

Add all ingredients to a 4-quart slow cooker. Cover and cook on low heat for 8 hours.

PER SERVING | Calories: 199 | Fat: 1 g | Protein: 11 g | Sodium: 488 mg | Fiber: 15 g | Carbohydrates: 38 g | Sugar: 10 g

Garden Vegetable Chili

A true garden vegetable recipe requires some flexibility, since all ingredients aren't available year round, and you should use what's actually growing in your garden.

INGREDIENTS | SERVES 8

1 large onion, diced

3 cloves garlic, minced

1 large green bell pepper, chopped

2 cups chopped zucchini

1½ cups corn kernels

1 (28-ounce) can diced tomatoes

2 cups Vegetable Broth (see Chapter 3)

1 (15-ounce) can kidney beans, drained

1 (15-ounce) can pinto beans, drained

1 (15-ounce) can cannellini beans, drained

2 tablespoons chili powder

1 teaspoon cumin

1 teaspoon dried oregano

1 teaspoon salt

¼ teaspoon black pepper

Add all ingredients to a 4-quart slow cooker. Cover and cook on low heat for 6 hours.

PER SERVING | Calories: 229 | Fat: 2.5 g | Protein: 10 g | Sodium: 548 mg | Fiber: 10 g | Carbohydrates: 35 g | Sugar: 5.5 g

Selecting What's in Season

In the summer, bell peppers, corn, green beans, and okra are in season and would be delicious additions to this recipe. In the winter, cauliflower, parsnips, and winter squash may be in season and would be good, too.

Pumpkin Chili

Pumpkin is typically complemented by sugar, cinnamon, and other earthy spices, but it also works well with a dash of heat, like chili powder.

INGREDIENTS | SERVES 6

2 tablespoons olive oil

1 onion, diced

2 (14-ounce) cans tomatoes

1 cup Vegetable Broth (see Chapter 3)

1 pumpkin, rind and seeds removed, flesh cut into ½-inch chunks

1 (14-ounce) can white beans, drained

2 tablespoons chili powder

3 teaspoons cumin

1 teaspoon salt

½ teaspoon black pepper

1. Add the oil to a 4-quart slow cooker and sauté the onion on medium-high heat for 3–5 minutes.

2. Add the rest of the ingredients and cook on low heat for 6 hours.

PER SERVING | Calories: 143 | Fat: 6 g | Protein: 5.5 g | Sodium: 801 mg | Fiber: 6 g | Carbohydrates: 19 g | Sugar: 6 g

CHAPTER 6

Sauces

Red Pepper Coulis

This versatile sauce can be tossed with ingredients such as cooked pasta or gnocchi, or even enjoyed as a dip or spread.

INGREDIENTS | SERVES 6

2 tablespoons olive oil

2 shallots, minced

2 red bell peppers, diced

2 cloves garlic, minced

1 cup Vegetable Broth (see Chapter 3)

¼ cup plain unsweetened soymilk

¼ teaspoon salt

⅛ teaspoon black pepper

1. Add the oil to a 4-quart slow cooker and sauté the shallots and red peppers on medium-high heat for 3–5 minutes. Add the garlic and sauté for 1 minute more.

2. Add the rest of the ingredients and cook on medium-high heat for 2 hours.

PER SERVING | Calories: 75 | Fat: 5 g | Protein: 1 g | Sodium: 106 mg | Fiber: 1.5 g | Carbohydrates: 7 g | Sugar: 4 g

What Is a Coulis?

A coulis is a thick sauce made from puréed fruits or vegetables. In this recipe, the slow cooking eliminates the need for puréeing because the peppers cook down until they are very soft.

Bolognese

If you'd like to add a protein punch to this sauce,
toss in 1 cup cooked white beans before cooking.

INGREDIENTS | SERVES 6

2 tablespoons olive oil

1 onion, diced

½ cup chopped celery

½ cup chopped carrots

3 cloves garlic, minced

2 (14-ounce) cans tomatoes, crushed

1 lemon, juiced

1 bunch parsley, chopped

1 teaspoon salt

½ teaspoon black pepper

1. Add the oil to a 4-quart slow cooker and sauté the onion, celery, and carrots on medium-high heat for 3–5 minutes. Add the garlic and sauté for 1 minute more.

2. Add the rest of the ingredients and cook on low heat for 4 hours.

PER SERVING | Calories: 90 | Fat: 5 g | Protein: 2.5 g | Sodium: 611 mg | Fiber: 3 g | Carbohydrates: 11 g | Sugar: 5 g

Tomatillo Sauce

Tomatillos look like small green tomatoes,
but they are actually related to the gooseberry.

INGREDIENTS | SERVES 4

12 tomatillos, husked

Water for cooking

1 onion, diced

2 garlic cloves, minced

1 jalapeño, seeded and minced

½ tablespoon chopped, fresh cilantro

1 teaspoon salt

1. Place the tomatillos in a 4-quart slow cooker with enough water to cover them. Set the slow cooker to high and allow the tomatillos to cook for 1–2 hours or until tender. Drain the tomatillos.

2. Place the tomatillos, onion, garlic, jalapeño, cilantro, and salt in a food processor and purée. Place the mixture in a bowl and add enough water until it has the consistency of a sauce.

PER SERVING | Calories: 47 | Fat: 0 g | Protein: 2 g | Sodium: 600 mg | Fiber: 3 g | Carbohydrates: 10 g | Sugar: 6 g

Chunky Tomato Sauce

When tomatoes are in season, try replacing the canned diced tomatoes in this recipe for 1 cup fresh Roma tomatoes.

INGREDIENTS | SERVES 6

2 tablespoons olive oil
1 onion, diced
4 cloves garlic, minced
1 teaspoon dried oregano
1 teaspoon dried parsley
1 teaspoon dried basil
1 lemon, juiced
½ cup water
1 (14-ounce) can diced tomatoes
1 (14-ounce) can crushed tomatoes
2 teaspoons sugar
1 teaspoon salt
½ teaspoon black pepper

1. Add the oil to a 4-quart slow cooker and sauté the onion on medium-high heat for 3–5 minutes. Add the garlic and sauté for 1 minute more.

2. Add the rest of the ingredients and cook on low heat for 6 hours.

PER SERVING | Calories: 81 | Fat: 5 g | Protein: 1.5 g | Sodium: 582 mg | Fiber: 2 g | Carbohydrates: 10 g | Sugar: 5.5 g

Crushed Tomatoes

Crushed tomatoes vary greatly by brand—some are thick, like a paste, and others are quite watery. When using crushed tomatoes in combination with other tomatoes, choose a thicker blend of crushed tomatoes.

Sun-Dried Tomato Sauce

Although sun-dried tomatoes lose over 90 percent of their weight when they are being dried in the sun, they maintain most of their nutritional value.

INGREDIENTS | SERVES 6

¼ cup Earth Balance Original Buttery Spread

¼ cup white flour

3½ cups plain unsweetened soymilk

1 cup chopped sun-dried tomatoes

1 tablespoon vegan Worcestershire sauce

1 teaspoon salt

¼ teaspoon black pepper

1. Set a 4-quart slow cooker to medium high and add the Earth Balance. Once the Earth Balance has melted, slowly stir in the flour to create a roux. Once the roux is created, whisk in the soymilk until smooth.

2. Add the rest of the ingredients and continue cooking on low heat for 2 hours, stirring occasionally.

PER SERVING | Calories: 170 | Fat: 10 g | Protein: 5 g | Sodium: 583 mg | Fiber: 1 g | Carbohydrates: 14 g | Sugar: 6 g

Sun-Dried at Home

You can make homemade sun-dried tomatoes by, you guessed it, halving tomatoes and leaving them out to dry in the sun for about a week. Other methods are available too, such as using the oven or a dehydrator.

White Wine–Dill Sauce

Toss this sauce with cooked angel hair pasta, and enjoy the rest of the wine with dinner.

INGREDIENTS | SERVES 6

¼ cup Earth Balance Original Buttery Spread

¼ cup white flour

3½ cups plain unsweetened soymilk

¼ cup white wine

1 teaspoon dried dill weed

1 tablespoon vegan Worcestershire sauce

1 teaspoon salt

¼ teaspoon black pepper

1. Set the slow cooker to medium high and add the Earth Balance. Allow the Earth Balance to melt while slowly stirring in the flour to create a roux. Once the roux is created, whisk in the soymilk until smooth.

2. Add the rest of the ingredients and continue cooking on medium-high heat for 2 hours, stirring occasionally.

PER SERVING | Calories: 173 | Fat: 10 g | Protein: 5 g | Sodium: 582 mg | Fiber: 1 g | Carbohydrates: 13 g | Sugar: 6 g

Carolina Barbecue Sauce

This sauce has a more acidic taste than the sweeter, mainstream, ketchup-based sauces.

INGREDIENTS | SERVES 6

¼ cup Earth Balance Original Buttery Spread

1 cup apple cider vinegar

⅓ cup brown sugar

1 tablespoon molasses

1 tablespoon mustard

2 teaspoons vegan Worcestershire sauce

⅛ teaspoon cayenne pepper

Add all of the ingredients to a 4-quart slow cooker and cook on medium-high heat for 1 hour, stirring occasionally.

PER SERVING | Calories: 135 | Fat: 7 g | Protein: 0 g | Sodium: 143 mg | Fiber: 0 g | Carbohydrates: 15 g | Sugar: 14 g

Red Wine Reduction

*Try using bolder wines, such as merlot, for heavier dishes and
less bold wines, such as pinot noir, for lighter dishes.*

INGREDIENTS | SERVES 4

2 tablespoons olive oil

1 shallot, minced

2 cloves garlic, minced

1 cup red wine

1 cup Vegetable Broth (see Chapter 3)

¼ cup Earth Balance Original Buttery Spread

1. Add the oil to a 4-quart slow cooker and sauté the shallot on medium-high heat for 3 minutes. Add the garlic and sauté for 1 minute more.

2. Add the remaining ingredients and cook on medium-high heat until the sauce has reduced by half, approximately 1–2 hours.

PER SERVING | Calories: 227 | Fat: 18 g | Protein: 0 g | Sodium: 136 mg | Fiber: 0 g | Carbohydrates: 5 g | Sugar: 2 g

Slow-Roasted Garlic and Tomato Sauce

Canned, diced tomatoes are a good substitute for fresh, vine-ripened tomatoes when fresh tomatoes are not in season.

INGREDIENTS | SERVES 6

2 tablespoons olive oil

2½ pounds fresh, vine-ripened tomatoes, peeled and diced

1 teaspoon dried parsley

1 teaspoon dried basil

1 tablespoon balsamic vinegar

½ teaspoon granulated cane sugar

¼ teaspoon of salt

¼ teaspoon freshly ground black pepper

3 heads roasted garlic, cloves removed from peel

Roasting Garlic

Roast whole heads of garlic by cutting off the top quarter, drizzling with olive oil, and then wrapping in aluminum foil. Cook in an oven preheated to 400°F for about 45 minutes.

Add all ingredients to a 4-quart slow cooker. Cover and cook on low for 3–4 hours.

PER SERVING (½ CUP) | Calories: 175 | Fat: 7.5 g | Protein: 5.2 g | Sodium: 21.5 mg | Fiber: 4 g | Carbohydrates: 25.5 g | Sugar: 8 g

Vegan Alfredo Sauce

Top cooked fettuccine with this updated version of a classic sauce.

INGREDIENTS | SERVES 8

1 cup raw cashews

1 cup water

½ cup unsweetened soymilk

3 cups Vegetable Broth (see Chapter 3)

Juice of ½ lemon

½ cup nutritional yeast

1 teaspoon mustard

2 cloves garlic, minced

2 teaspoons salt

1 teaspoon pepper

1. In a blender, place the cashews, water, and soymilk. Process until very smooth.

2. In a 4-quart slow cooker, pour the blended cashew sauce and all remaining ingredients and stir well. Cover and cook over low heat for 1 hour.

PER SERVING | Calories: 185.5 | Fat: 12.6 g | Protein: 6.3 g | Sodium: 638 mg | Fiber: 2 g | Carbohydrates: 13 g | Sugar: 4 g

Cooking with Cashews

Cashews are an excellent ingredient to use when you want to create a creamy vegan dish, but be sure to use raw cashews, not roasted or cooked in any other way. Also remember that nuts are high in calories and fat, so they should be consumed in small quantities.

Easy Peanut Sauce

Choose a peanut butter that is free of added flavors and is as natural as possible so that it won't distort the flavors in your dish.

INGREDIENTS | SERVES 6

1 cup smooth peanut butter
4 tablespoons maple syrup
½ cup sesame oil
1 teaspoon cayenne pepper
1½ teaspoons cumin
1 teaspoon garlic powder
1½ teaspoons salt
2 cups water

1. In a blender, add all ingredients except for the water. Blend as you slowly add the water until you reach the desired consistency.

2. Pour the sauce into a 2-quart slow cooker and cook over low heat for 1 hour.

PER SERVING (½ CUP) | Calories: 452 | Fat: 40 g | Protein: 11 g | Sodium: 792 mg | Fiber: 3 g | Carbohydrates: 18 g | Sugar: 12 g

Uses for Peanut Sauce

Peanut sauce can be used to dress Asian noodles such as udon or soba noodles. It may also be used as a dipping sauce for steamed broccoli or spring rolls.

Mole

Just like barbecue sauce in the United States, mole sauce recipes vary greatly by region, and no two are exactly the same.

INGREDIENTS | SERVES 6

2 tablespoons olive oil

½ onion, finely diced

3 garlic cloves, minced

1 teaspoon ground cumin

¼ teaspoon ground cinnamon

¼ teaspoon ground coriander

1 tablespoon chili powder

2 chipotles in adobo, seeded and minced

1 teaspoon salt

4 cups Vegetable Broth (see Chapter 3)

1 ounce vegan dark chocolate, chopped

1. In a sauté pan over medium heat, add the oil, onion, and garlic, and sauté about 3 minutes. Add the cumin, cinnamon, and coriander, and sauté for 1 minute.

2. Transfer the sautéed mixture to a 4-quart slow cooker. Add the chili powder, chipotles, and salt, then whisk in the vegetable broth. Finally, add the chocolate.

3. Cover and cook over medium heat for 2 hours.

PER SERVING (½ CUP) | Calories: 163 | Fat: 9.6 g | Protein: 2 g | Sodium: 407 mg | Fiber: 4.5 g | Carbohydrates: 20 g | Sugar: 10 g

Coconut Curry Sauce

Red curry paste is ideal for this recipe, but any variety will do.

INGREDIENTS | SERVES 6

1 (14-ounce) can coconut milk

1 cup Vegetable Broth (see Chapter 3)

1 teaspoon soy sauce

1 tablespoon curry paste

1 tablespoon lime juice

2 cloves garlic, minced

½ teaspoon salt

¼ cup chopped cilantro

1. In a 4-quart slow cooker, add all ingredients except cilantro. Cover and cook on low heat for 2 hours.

2. Add the chopped cilantro and cook for an additional 30 minutes.

PER SERVING (½ CUP) | Calories: 214 | Fat: 21 g | Protein: 2.7 g | Sodium: 255 mg | Fiber: 1 g | Carbohydrates: 7 g | Sugar: 1.5 g

Vegetables

Parsnip Purée

Parsnips are long, white root vegetables related to carrots. Due to the starchiness of their texture, they can frequently be used in place of potatoes.

INGREDIENTS | SERVES 6

5 medium parsnips, peeled and chopped
½ cup Vegetable Broth (see Chapter 3)
½ cup unsweetened soymilk
1 teaspoon salt
1 tablespoon Earth Balance Original Buttery Spread

1. Add the parsnips, Vegetable Broth, soymilk, and salt to a 4-quart slow cooker. Cover and cook over low heat for 4 hours.

2. Allow the parsnips to cool slightly, then use an immersion blender to process, or use a blender or food processor and blend in batches.

3. Return to the slow cooker, add the Earth Balance, and heat until melted.

PER SERVING | Calories: 51 | Fat: 2.6 g | Protein: 1 g | Sodium: 411 mg | Fiber: 1.4 g | Carbohydrates: 6 g | Sugar: 2.7 g

Citrusy Beets

Beets can be served as a warm side dish or a chilled salad over a bed of greens.

INGREDIENTS | SERVES 4

12 baby beets, halved, ends trimmed
1 cup orange juice
Juice of ½ lime
¼ red onion, sliced
½ teaspoon pepper

Add all ingredients to a 2-quart or 4-quart slow cooker and cook on low for 4 hours.

PER SERVING | Calories: 142 | Fat: 1 g | Protein: 5 g | Sodium: 194 mg | Fiber: 7.5 g | Carbohydrates: 32 g | Sugar: 22 g

Creamed Spinach

*Fresh spinach reduces greatly when cooked, so to get a bigger bang
for your buck, use frozen spinach when possible.*

INGREDIENTS | SERVES 6

1 tablespoon Earth Balance Original
Buttery Spread
1 clove garlic, minced
1 tablespoon flour
1 cup unsweetened soymilk
½ teaspoon salt
½ teaspoon crushed red pepper
¼ teaspoon dried sage
1 (12-ounce) package frozen spinach,
thawed

1. Melt the Earth Balance in a 2-quart slow cooker over medium heat. Add the garlic and cook for 2 minutes before stirring in the flour to form a roux.

2. Slowly pour in the soymilk and whisk until all lumps are removed.

3. Add all remaining ingredients. Stir and cook over low heat for 1–2 hours.

PER SERVING | Calories: 61 | Fat: 3 g | Protein: 3.6 g | Sodium: 281 mg | Fiber: 2 g | Carbohydrates: 6 g | Sugar: 2 g

Variations

You can simplify this recipe by going with a simple butter or margarine sauce that is flavored with salt, pepper, and sage, or you can make this savory dish even richer by adding a sprinkling of vegan cheese such as Daiya Mozzarella Style Shreds.

Eggplant Caponata

*Serve this on small slices of Italian bread as an appetizer
or use as a filling in sandwiches or wraps.*

INGREDIENTS | SERVES 8

2 (1-pound) eggplants
1 teaspoon olive oil
1 red onion, diced
4 cloves garlic, minced
1 stalk celery, diced
2 tomatoes, diced
2 tablespoons nonpareil capers
2 tablespoons toasted pine nuts
1 teaspoon red pepper flakes
¼ cup red wine vinegar

Capers

Capers are found on a flowering bush, and the flower bud is what is commonly called the "caper." They are often pickled and used in a variety of sauces and salads.

1. Pierce the eggplants with a fork. Cook on high in a 4- or 6-quart slow cooker for 2 hours.

2. Allow to cool. Peel off the skin. Slice each in half and remove the seeds. Discard the skin and seeds.

3. Place the pulp in a food processor. Pulse until smooth. Set aside.

4. Heat the oil in a nonstick skillet. Sauté the onion, garlic, and celery until the onion is soft, about 5 minutes.

5. Add the eggplant and tomatoes. Sauté 3 minutes.

6. Return to the slow cooker and add the capers, pine nuts, red pepper flakes, and vinegar. Stir. Cook on low for 30 minutes. Stir prior to serving.

PER SERVING | Calories: 54 | Fat: 1 g | Protein: 2 g | Sodium: 73 mg | Fiber: 5 g | Carbohydrates: 10 g | Sugar: 4 g

Caramelized Onions

Caramelized onions are a great addition to roasts, dips, and sandwiches.

INGREDIENTS | SERVES 8

4 pounds Vidalia or other sweet onions

3 tablespoons Earth Balance Original Buttery Spread

1 tablespoon balsamic vinegar

Storing Caramelized Onions

Store the onions in an airtight container. They will keep for up to 2 weeks refrigerated or up to 6 months frozen. If frozen, defrost overnight in the refrigerator before using.

1. Peel and slice the onions into ¼-inch slices. Separate them into rings.

2. Place the onions into a 4-quart slow cooker. Scatter chunks of the Earth Balance over top of the onions and drizzle with balsamic vinegar. Cover and cook on low for 10 hours.

3. If after 10 hours the onions are wet, turn the slow cooker up to high and cook uncovered for an additional 30 minutes, or until the liquid evaporates.

PER SERVING (2 TABLESPOONS) | Calories: 35 | Fat: 1 g | Protein: 1 g | Sodium: 0 mg | Fiber: <1 g | Carbohydrates: 6 g | Sugar: 3 g

Creamed Corn

For this recipe, choose frozen corn that is free of salt or added flavors.

INGREDIENTS | SERVES 4

1 (16-ounce) bag frozen corn kernels

½ cup unsweetened soymilk

¼ cup Earth Balance Original Buttery Spread

½ teaspoon salt

¼ teaspoon pepper

1. Add all ingredients to a 4-quart slow cooker. Cover and cook on high heat for 3 hours.

2. Allow to cool slightly, then pour ¼ of the corn into a blender and pulse 1–2 times. Return to the slow cooker and stir before serving.

PER SERVING | Calories: 219 | Fat: 13 g | Protein: 4.5 g | Sodium: 313 mg | Fiber: 2.7 g | Carbohydrates: 1 g | Sugar: 1.6 g

Rosemary-Thyme Green Beans

In this recipe, the slow cooker acts like a steamer,
resulting in tender, crisp green beans.

INGREDIENTS | SERVES 4

1 pound green beans

1 tablespoon minced, fresh rosemary

1 teaspoon minced, fresh thyme

2 tablespoons lemon juice

2 tablespoons water

1. Place all ingredients into a 2-quart slow cooker. Stir to distribute the spices evenly.

2. Cook on low for 1½ hours, or until the green beans are tender. Stir before serving.

PER SERVING | Calories: 40 | Fat: 0 g | Protein: 2 g | Sodium: 5 mg | Fiber: 4 g | Carbohydrates: 9 g | Sugar: 4 g

Herb-Stuffed Tomatoes

Serve these Italian-influenced stuffed tomatoes
with a simple salad for an easy, light meal.

INGREDIENTS | SERVES 4

4 large tomatoes

1 cup cooked quinoa

1 stalk celery, minced

1 tablespoon minced, fresh garlic

2 tablespoons minced, fresh oregano

2 tablespoons minced, fresh Italian parsley

1 teaspoon dried chervil

1 teaspoon fennel seeds

¾ cup water

1. Cut out the core of each tomato and discard. Scoop out the seeds, leaving the walls of the tomato intact.

2. In a small bowl, stir together the quinoa, celery, garlic, and spices. Divide evenly among the 4 tomatoes.

3. Place the filled tomatoes in a single layer in an oval 4-quart slow cooker. Pour the water into the bottom of the slow cooker. Cook on low for 4 hours.

PER SERVING | Calories: 191 | Fat: 2 g | Protein: 7 g | Sodium: 30 mg | Fiber: 4.5 g | Carbohydrates: 29 g | Sugar: 5 g

Ratatouille

Ratatouille made in the slow cooker comes out surprisingly crisp and tender.

INGREDIENTS | SERVES 4

1 onion, roughly chopped

1 eggplant, sliced horizontally

2 medium zucchini, sliced

1 cubanelle pepper, sliced

3 tomatoes, cut into wedges

2 tablespoons minced, fresh basil

2 tablespoons minced, fresh Italian parsley

¼ teaspoon salt

½ teaspoon freshly ground black pepper

3 ounces tomato paste

¼ cup water

1. Place the onion, eggplant, zucchini, pepper, and tomatoes into a 4-quart slow cooker. Sprinkle with basil, parsley, salt, and pepper.

2. In a small bowl, whisk the tomato paste and water together. Pour the mixture over the vegetables. Stir.

3. Cook on low for 4 hours, or until the eggplant and zucchini are fork-tender.

PER SERVING | Calories: 110 | Fat: 1 g | Protein: 5 g | Sodium: 330 mg | Fiber: 8 g | Carbohydrates: 24 g | Sugar: 13 g

Cubanelle Peppers

Cubanelles look very similar to banana peppers and are similar in taste and heat, but they are two different varieties. Cubanelles can be mild to somewhat spicy and, like banana peppers, are often pickled.

Stuffed Eggplant

This easy vegan dish is a complete meal in itself.

INGREDIENTS | SERVES 2

1 (1-pound) eggplant
½ teaspoon olive oil
2 tablespoons minced red onion
1 clove garlic, minced
⅓ cup cooked rice
1 tablespoon chopped, fresh parsley
¼ cup corn kernels
¼ cup diced crimini mushrooms
1 (15-ounce) can diced tomatoes

1. Preheat oven to 375°F.

2. Slice the eggplant in 2 equal halves, lengthwise. Use an ice cream scoop to take out the seeds. Place on a baking sheet, skin side down. Bake for 8 minutes. Allow to cool slightly.

3. Place the oil in an a small skillet over medium heat. Add the onions and garlic, and sauté until softened, about 3 minutes.

4. In a medium bowl, stir the onions, garlic, rice, parsley, corn, and mushrooms. Divide evenly between the eggplant halves.

5. Pour the tomatoes onto the bottom of an oval 4- or 6-quart slow cooker. Place the eggplant halves side by side on top of the tomatoes. Cook on low for 3 hours.

6. Remove and plate the eggplants. Drizzle with tomato sauce.

PER SERVING | Calories: 190 | Fat: 3.5 g | Protein: 8 g | Sodium: 807 mg | Fiber: 10 g | Carbohydrates: 41 g | Sugar: 12 g

Spiced "Baked" Eggplant

Serve this as a main dish over rice or as a side dish as is.

INGREDIENTS | SERVES 4

1 pound eggplant, cubed
⅓ cup sliced onion
½ teaspoon red pepper flakes
½ teaspoon crushed rosemary
¼ cup lemon juice

Place all ingredients in a 1½- or 2-quart slow cooker. Cook on low for 3 hours, or until the eggplant is tender.

PER SERVING | Calories: 40 | Fat: 0 g | Protein: 1 g | Sodium: 6 mg | Fiber: 4 g | Carbohydrates: 9 g | Sugar: 3.5 g

Cold Snap

Take care not to put a cold ceramic slow cooker insert directly into the slow cooker. The sudden shift in temperature can cause it to crack. If you want to prepare your ingredients the night before use, refrigerate them in reusable containers, not in the insert.

Stewed Tomatoes

For an Italian variation, add basil and Italian parsley.

INGREDIENTS | SERVES 6

4 cups diced Roma tomatoes
1 tablespoon minced onion
1 stalk celery, diced
½ teaspoon oregano
½ teaspoon thyme

Place all ingredients into a 2-quart slow cooker. Stir. Cook on low up to 8 hours.

PER SERVING | Calories: 23 | Fat: 0 g | Protein: 1 g | Sodium: 11 g | Fiber: 2 g | Carbohydrates: 5 g | Sugar: 3 g

Tomato Varieties

Small tomatoes, such as Roma tomatoes or cherry tomatoes, are best for this recipe. Avoid large tomatoes that are used for their large slices, such as beefsteak.

Zucchini Ragout

A ragout is either a main-dish stew or a sauce. This one can be served as either.

INGREDIENTS | SERVES 6

5 ounces fresh spinach

3 medium zucchini, diced

½ cup diced red onion

2 stalks celery, diced

2 carrots, diced

1 parsnip, diced

3 tablespoons tomato paste

¼ cup water

1 teaspoon freshly ground black pepper

¼ teaspoon kosher salt

1 tablespoon minced, fresh basil

1 tablespoon minced, fresh Italian parsley

1 tablespoon minced, fresh oregano

Place all ingredients into a 4-quart slow cooker. Stir. Cook on low for 4 hours. Stir before serving.

PER SERVING | Calories: 60 | Fat: 0 g | Protein: 2 g | Sodium: 220 mg | Fiber: 3 g | Carbohydrates: 10 g | Sugar: 3 g

Saving on Herbs

The cost of herbs can add up quickly, but you can save a little money by shopping at a farmers' market or buying a blend of spices (an Italian blend would work well in this recipe) instead of buying each individually.

Moroccan Root Vegetables

*These Moroccan-spiced root vegetables are delicious
when served with couscous and a yogurt or vegan side salad.*

INGREDIENTS | SERVES 8

1 pound parsnips, peeled and diced
1 pound turnips, peeled and diced
2 medium onions, chopped
1 pound carrots, peeled and diced
6 dried apricots, chopped
4 pitted prunes, chopped
1 teaspoon ground turmeric
1 teaspoon ground cumin
½ teaspoon ground ginger
½ teaspoon ground cinnamon
¼ teaspoon ground cayenne pepper
1 tablespoon dried parsley
1 tablespoon dried cilantro
2 cups Vegetable Broth (see Chapter 3)
1 teaspoon salt

1. Add the parsnips, turnips, onions, carrots, apricots, prunes, turmeric, cumin, ginger, cinnamon, cayenne pepper, parsley, and cilantro to a 4-quart slow cooker.

2. Pour in the Vegetable Broth and salt.

3. Cover and cook on low for 9 hours, or until the vegetables are cooked through.

PER SERVING | Calories: 125 | Fat: 0.6 g | Protein: 2.7 g | Sodium: 302 mg | Fiber: 6 g | Carbohydrates: 30 g | Sugar: 14 g

Meatless Moussaka

If you get your eggplant at the supermarket and suspect that it's been waxed, peel it before dicing it and adding it to the slow cooker.

INGREDIENTS | SERVES 8

¾ cup dry brown or yellow lentils, rinsed and drained

2 large potatoes, peeled and diced

1 cup water

1 stalk celery, diced fine

1 medium sweet onion, peeled and diced

3 cloves garlic, minced

½ teaspoon salt

¼ teaspoon ground cinnamon

¼ teaspoon freshly ground nutmeg

¼ teaspoon freshly ground black pepper

¼ teaspoon dried basil

¼ teaspoon dried oregano

¼ teaspoon dried parsley

1 medium eggplant, diced

12 baby carrots, each cut into 3 pieces

2 cups diced Roma tomatoes

1 (8-ounce) package vegan cream cheese, softened

1. Add the lentils, potatoes, water, celery, onion, garlic, salt, cinnamon, nutmeg, pepper, basil, oregano, and parsley to a 4-quart slow cooker. Stir. Top with eggplant and carrots.

2. Cover and cook on low for 6 hours, or until the lentils are cooked through.

3. Stir in the tomatoes and add a dollop of vegan cream cheese over lentil mixture. Cover and cook on low for an additional 30 minutes.

PER SERVING | Calories: 235 | Fat: 10 g | Protein: 8.6 g | Sodium: 333 mg | Fiber: 7 g | Carbohydrates: 29 g | Sugar: 6 g

Traditional Moussaka

Moussaka is traditionally made with minced meat, but you can easily veganize the Greek and Arabic dish by using an abundance of vegetables instead. It can be served either warm or cold.

Curried Cauliflower

Heating herbs and spices before adding them to water intensifies the flavor.

INGREDIENTS | SERVES 6

1 tablespoon olive oil
¼ cup finely diced onion
1½ teaspoons curry powder
½ teaspoon cumin
½ teaspoon coriander
1 teaspoon chili powder
1 teaspoon salt
1 cup diced tomatoes
1 cup water
1 head cauliflower, chopped

1. Heat the olive oil in the bottom of a 4-quart slow cooker set to medium heat. Add the onion and cook for 5 minutes.

2. Add the curry powder, cumin, coriander, chili powder, salt, and tomatoes, and stir until well combined.

3. Add the water and cauliflower to the spice mixture in the slow cooker and stir until the cauliflower is coated. Cover and cook over medium heat for about 3 hours.

PER SERVING | Calories: 56 | Fat: 3 g | Protein: 2 g | Sodium: 430 mg | Fiber: 3 g | Carbohydrates: 7 g | Sugar: 3 g

Braised Baby Bok Choy

Bok choy is also known as Chinese cabbage. Baby bok choy is simply a smaller, more tender version of mature bok choy.

INGREDIENTS | SERVES 6

2 tablespoons soy sauce
2 tablespoons apple cider vinegar
1 tablespoon vegetable oil
½ teaspoon garlic powder
1 teaspoon crushed red pepper flakes
3 heads baby bok choy, halved lengthwise

1. In a small bowl, whisk together all ingredients, except for the bok choy.

2. Place the bok choy in a 4-quart slow cooker, then pour the soy sauce mixture over the bok choy. Cover and cook on low heat for 3 hours.

PER SERVING | Calories: 102 | Fat: 5 g | Protein: 7 g | Sodium: 573 mg | Fiber: 3 g | Carbohydrates: 10 g | Sugar: 5.6 g

Mushroom and Olive Blend

Try serving on top of toasted baguette slices, on pasta, or as a savory side dish.

INGREDIENTS | SERVES 6

2 tablespoons Earth Balance Original Buttery Spread
1 clove garlic, minced
½ cup sliced shiitake mushrooms
½ cup sliced oyster mushrooms
½ cup chopped hen of the woods mushrooms
¼ cup pitted and sliced kalamata olives
½ teaspoon salt
¼ teaspoon pepper

Add all ingredients to a 2-quart slow cooker. Cover and cook on low heat for 2 hours. Stir occasionally to make sure the butter or margarine is coating the mushrooms.

PER SERVING | Calories: 44 | Fat: 4 g | Protein: 0.7 g | Sodium: 199 mg | Fiber: 1 g | Carbohydrates: 2 g | Sugar: 0.4 g

Mushroom Varieties

Hen of the woods mushrooms are also called maitake mushrooms, and they grow in clusters. If you can't find this variety, you can substitute with a ½ cup more shiitake or oyster mushrooms.

Summer Squash Casserole

*The cornstarch, water, and soymilk act as the binding agent in this casserole,
and the nutritional yeast gives it a hint of cheesy flavor.*

INGREDIENTS | SERVES 8

2 tablespoons Earth Balance Original Buttery Spread

½ white onion, diced

2 cloves garlic, minced

2 teaspoons cornstarch

2 tablespoons water

4 cups diced yellow squash

½ cup diced button mushrooms

1 cup unsweetened soymilk

¼ cup nutritional yeast

½ teaspoon salt

¼ teaspoon black pepper

30 Ritz Crackers, crushed

Butter Crackers

Golden, round crackers are often called "butter" crackers, but one of the most popular brands, Ritz Crackers, contains no butter at all. There are several vegan butter crackers available in stores. Just be sure to read the label before purchasing.

1. Melt the Earth Balance in a 4-quart slow cooker over high heat. Add the onion and sauté for 3 minutes. Add the garlic and sauté for an additional minute. Reduce heat to low.

2. Combine the cornstarch and water in a small bowl and whisk until all lumps have been removed.

3. Add cornstarch mixture, squash, mushrooms, soymilk, nutritional yeast, salt, pepper, and half of the crackers to the slow cooker, and stir until well combined. Top with the remaining crackers.

4. Cover and cook on low heat for 4 hours.

PER SERVING | Calories: 132 | Fat: 6 g | Protein: 5 g | Sodium: 619 mg | Fiber: 1.5 g | Carbohydrates: 14 g | Sugar: 5 g

Basic Brussels

Overcooking Brussels sprouts is a common culprit for ruining the flavor. Be sure to cook until just done, which is soft enough to stick a fork into but not mushy, and don't use more liquid than is needed.

INGREDIENTS | SERVES 6

1 pound Brussels sprouts, trimmed and halved

2 tablespoons Earth Balance Original Buttery Spread

3 tablespoons water

½ teaspoon salt

¼ teaspoon pepper

Place all ingredients in a 2-quart slow cooker. Cover and cook on high heat for 2½ hours.

PER SERVING | Calories: 66 | Fat: 4 g | Protein: 2.5 g | Sodium: 259 mg | Fiber: 3 g | Carbohydrates: 7 g | Sugar: 1.5 g

Marinated Artichokes

Marinated artichokes can be stored in the refrigerator for about 1 week, or if you jar them, about 2 months.

INGREDIENTS | SERVES 4

2 (9-ounce) boxes fresh artichoke hearts

½ cup olive oil

¼ cup cider vinegar

2 tablespoons lemon juice

3 bay leaves

1 teaspoon dried oregano

½ teaspoon salt

½ teaspoon crushed red pepper flakes

Combine all ingredients in a 2-quart slow cooker and stir well. Cover and cook over low heat for 2 hours.

PER SERVING | Calories: 304 | Fat: 27 g | Protein: 4 g | Sodium: 416 mg | Fiber: 7 g | Carbohydrates: 14 g | Sugar: 1.5 g

Artichoke Barigoule

Canned or frozen artichokes are not a good substitute for the fresh artichokes in this dish because they will overcook very quickly.

INGREDIENTS | SERVES 6

6 artichoke hearts, quartered

2 carrots, finely diced

2 shallots, finely diced

3 cloves garlic, minced

2 lemons, juiced

½ cup white wine

½ cup water

¼ cup olive oil

1 sprig thyme

½ teaspoon salt

¼ cup chopped flat-leaf parsley

1. In a 2-quart slow cooker, place all ingredients except for the parsley. Stir well and cover. Cook on low heat for 4 hours.

2. Stir in the chopped parsley and serve.

PER SERVING | Calories: 201 | Fat: 10 g | Protein: 6 g | Sodium: 340 mg | Fiber: 10 g | Carbohydrates: 25 g | Sugar: 5 g

What Is Provençal?

Barigoule is a traditional Provençal dish, which means it hails from the Provence region in the south of France. The cuisine of Provence is influenced by its proximity to the Mediterranean Sea and is characterized by its use of seafood, olives, and garlic.

Mashed Kabocha Squash

*Kabocha is a type of Japanese squash that mashes
very easily when cooked. It also becomes quite fluffy!*

INGREDIENTS | SERVES 6

1 kabocha squash, peeled and cubed

1 cup water

3 tablespoons Earth Balance Original
Buttery Spread

1 teaspoon salt

¼ teaspoon black pepper

1. Add all ingredients to a 6-quart slow cooker. Cover and cook over low heat for 6–8 hours.

2. Mash the squash using a fork or masher and stir until creamy.

PER SERVING | Calories: 56 | Fat: 6 g | Protein: 0 g | Sodium: 460 mg | Fiber: 0 g | Carbohydrates: 1 g | Sugar: 1 g

Lemon and Oil Green Beans

*This dish can be served warm, or for a summery treat,
chill for 2 hours and serve cold.*

INGREDIENTS | SERVES 4

¼ cup water

2 tablespoons olive oil

1 lemon, juiced

½ teaspoons salt

1 pound green beans, trimmed

1. Add the water, olive oil, lemon juice, and salt to a 4-quart slow cooker and stir.

2. Add the green beans and toss until well coated. Cover and cook over low heat for 2 hours.

PER SERVING | Calories: 110 | Fat: 7 g | Protein: 2 g | Sodium: 302 mg | Fiber: 3 g | Carbohydrates: 9 g | Sugar: 4 g

How to Trim

Green beans have one tougher end and one pretty tapered end. To trim a pile of beans quickly, line up the beans with the tough ends all pointing in the same direction, and use a large knife to cut them off all at the same time. Leave the pretty tapered end intact.

Warm Jicama Slaw

Jicama is a crunchy root vegetable that is typically served cold, but it also works well in warm dishes because it retains its crunchy texture.

INGREDIENTS | SERVES 6

¼ cup lime juice
¼ cup water
¼ cup orange juice
2 tablespoons vegetable oil
1 teaspoon vinegar
1 teaspoon red pepper flakes
2 cups peeled and shredded jicama
1 cup shredded cabbage
1 cup peeled and shredded carrot

1. Combine the lime juice, water, orange juice, oil, vinegar, and red pepper flakes in a small bowl, and stir until well combined.

2. Add the jicama, cabbage, and carrots to a 4-quart slow cooker. Add the liquid and stir. Cover and cook over low heat for 1 hour.

PER SERVING | Calories: 75 | Fat: 5 g | Protein: 1 g | Sodium: 19 mg | Fiber: 3 g | Carbohydrates: 8 g | Sugar: 3 g

Slow Cooked Cabbage

Cabbage is an easy and inexpensive side dish that goes well as a side with barbecue seitan or tempeh.

INGREDIENTS | SERVES 6

1 cup shredded cabbage
½ white onion, sliced
4 cloves garlic, minced
2 tablespoons olive oil
½ teaspoon salt
¼ teaspoon pepper

Add all ingredients to a 6-quart slow cooker and toss. Cover and cook over low heat for 4 hours.

PER SERVING | Calories: 49 | Fat: 4.5 g | Protein: 0 g | Sodium: 199 mg | Fiber: 0.5 g | Carbohydrates: 2 g | Sugar: 1 g

In Season

Cabbage is at its peak during the fall and winter months. That makes it a suitable addition to hearty dishes such as root vegetable stews or potato dishes.

Stuffed Bell Peppers

The cuisine of Mexico inspired this version of stuffed bell peppers, but you can also prepare the versatile peppers with an Italian twist by replacing the chorizo and chili powder with chopped parsley, basil, and vegan Italian sausage.

INGREDIENTS | SERVES 4

1 cup crumbled soy chorizo
1 cup diced Roma tomatoes
¼ teaspoon garlic powder
1 teaspoon chili powder
½ teaspoon salt
½ cup diced red onion
3 cups plain dry bread crumbs
4 green bell peppers
½ cup shredded vegan Cheddar cheese

1. Combine all of the ingredients, except the bell peppers and vegan cheese, in a medium bowl and stir until well combined.

2. To prepare the bell peppers, cut the tops off of each pepper and scoop out the pulp and seeds. Stuff each pepper with ¼ of the bread crumb mixture.

3. Arrange the bell peppers so they are standing upright in a 4-quart slow cooker. Sprinkle with the vegan cheese, cover, and cook on low heat for 4–6 hours.

PER SERVING | Calories: 414 | Fat: 7 g | Protein: 18 g | Sodium: 930 mg | Fiber: 7 g | Carbohydrates: 69 g | Sugar: 11 g

Sesame Bok Choy

Mirin is a sweet rice wine that is commonly used in Asian recipes. Most recipes don't call for much because of the strong flavor, but it shouldn't be skipped. It adds sweetness and depth to the dish.

INGREDIENTS | SERVES 6

3 tablespoons sesame oil

1 tablespoon soy sauce

1 teaspoon mirin

1 clove garlic, minced

1 teaspoon lime juice

1 head bok choy, cut into 1-inch strips

1. In a small bowl, whisk together all ingredients, except for the bok choy.

2. Place the bok choy in a 4-quart slow cooker, then pour the soy sauce mixture over the bok choy. Cover and cook on low heat for 3 hours.

PER SERVING | Calories: 80 | Fat: 7 g | Protein: 2 g | Sodium: 204 | Fiber: 1.5 g | Carbohydrates: 3.5 g | Sugar: 2 g

Lime-Soaked Poblanos

Simple and fresh, this easy recipe can be used as the filling for tacos, burritos, or as a topping on a nopalitos (cactus) salad.

INGREDIENTS | SERVES 4

¼ cup lime juice

¼ cup water

2 cloves garlic, minced

2 tablespoons chopped, fresh cilantro

½ teaspoon salt

4 poblano peppers, seeded and sliced

Combine all of the ingredients in a 4-quart slow cooker and stir until well combined. Cover and cook on low heat for 4 hours.

PER SERVING | Calories: 29 | Fat: 0 g | Protein: 1 g | Sodium: 301 mg | Fiber: 2 g | Carbohydrates: 7 g | Sugar: 3 g

Chipotle Corn on the Cob

The corn husks from this recipe can be dried out and reused as a tamale casing.

INGREDIENTS | SERVES 6

6 ears corn, shucked

Water, as needed

3 tablespoons Earth Balance Original Buttery Spread

½ teaspoon chipotle powder

½ teaspoon salt

1. Place the corn in a 4-quart slow cooker and cover with water until it is 1-inch from the top of the slow cooker.

2. Cook on high heat for 2 hours.

3. While the corn is cooking, combine the Earth Balance, chipotle powder, and salt in a small bowl. When the corn is done cooking, rub a small spoonful of the Earth Balance mixture on each cob and then serve.

PER SERVING | Calories: 173 | Fat: 7 g | Protein: 4 g | Sodium: 271 mg | Fiber: 3.5 g | Carbohydrates: 29 g | Sugar: 4 g

CHAPTER 8

Potatoes

Southwestern Casserole

Serve it up taco style! You can scoop this casserole into warmed corn tortillas for an easy, hand-held serving option.

INGREDIENTS | SERVES 6

4 large red potatoes, diced

1 (15-ounce) can black beans, drained

1 large onion, diced

1 jalapeño, seeded and diced

1 tablespoon Earth Balance Original Buttery Spread

1 (15-ounce) can diced tomatoes

4 ounces button mushrooms, sliced

¼ teaspoon salt

¼ teaspoon pepper

¼ cup shredded vegan Cheddar cheese

1. In a 4-quart slow cooker, stir all ingredients together except the vegan cheese.

2. Cover and cook on low for 8–9 hours.

3. Stir in the cheese shortly before serving.

PER SERVING | Calories: 217 | Fat: 4 g | Protein: 9 g | Sodium: 445 mg | Fiber: 6 g | Carbohydrates: 38 g | Sugar: 6 g

Vegan Cheddar

There are several varieties of vegan Cheddar cheese for sale in grocery stores around the country, but the one that melts, stretches, and tastes the best is Daiya's Cheddar Style Shreds.

Potato Risotto

Finely diced potato replaces Arborio rice in this spin on a classic.
You can replace the spinach with peas if you like.

INGREDIENTS | SERVES 4

2 leeks (white part only)

¼ cup olive oil

3 sprigs fresh thyme, chopped

3 pounds russet potatoes, peeled and finely diced

2 cups dry white wine

5 cups Vegetable Broth (see Chapter 3)

1 teaspoon salt

¼ teaspoon black pepper

4 cups fresh spinach

1. Thinly slice the leeks crosswise into semicircles and rinse.

2. Add the olive oil to a 4-quart slow cooker and sauté the leeks on high heat until translucent, about 5–7 minutes.

3. Add the rest of the ingredients except for the spinach. Cover and cook on medium-high heat for 4 hours.

4. Mix the spinach into the risotto and continue cooking for 1 more hour.

PER SERVING | Calories: 580 | Fat: 12 g | Protein: 10 g | Sodium: 595 mg | Fiber: 7 g | Carbohydrates: 74 g | Sugar: 9 g

Sweet Potato Casserole

If you'd like to use fresh sweet potatoes in this casserole,
steam or roast them before using in the dish.

INGREDIENTS | SERVES 4

2 (18-ounce) cans sweet potatoes, drained and slightly mashed

1 cup unsweetened soymilk

½ cup melted Earth Balance Original Buttery Spread

½ cup sugar

1 teaspoon cinnamon

½ teaspoon nutmeg

½ cup chopped pecans

½ cup brown sugar

2 tablespoons flour

1. Add the slightly mashed sweet potatoes, soymilk, ¼ cup Earth Balance, white sugar, cinnamon, and nutmeg to a 4-quart slow cooker.

2. In a bowl, mix the pecans, brown sugar, flour, and remaining ¼ cup Earth Balance.

3. Pour the mixture over the top of the casserole. Cover and cook on low heat for 3–4 hours.

PER SERVING | Calories: 666 | Fat: 34 g | Protein: 8 g | Sodium: 181 mg | Fiber: 10 g | Carbohydrates: 96 g | Sugar: 64 g

Potatoes Paprikash

This Hungarian classic is the perfect spicy side dish to serve with a seitan roast.

INGREDIENTS | SERVES 8

1½ teaspoons olive oil

1 medium onion, halved and sliced

1 shallot, minced

4 cloves garlic, minced

½ teaspoon salt

½ teaspoon caraway seeds

¼ teaspoon freshly ground black pepper

1 teaspoon cayenne

3 tablespoons paprika

2 pounds red skin potatoes, thinly sliced

2 cups Vegetable Broth (see Chapter 3)

2 tablespoons tomato paste

½ cup vegan sour cream

Hungarian Cuisine

Hungarian food is very aromatic and can be quite heavy. It's most famous dishes are goulash, a meat and vegetable soup or stew, and paprikash.

1. In a small nonstick pan, heat the oil over medium heat. Add the onion, shallot, and garlic, and sauté for 1–2 minutes, or until they begin to soften. Add the salt, caraway seeds, pepper, cayenne, and paprika, and stir. Immediately remove from heat.

2. Add the onion mixture, potatoes, broth, and tomato paste to a 4-quart slow cooker. Stir to coat the potatoes evenly.

3. Cover and cook on high for 2½ hours, or until the potatoes are tender.

4. Turn off the heat and stir in the vegan sour cream.

PER SERVING | Calories: 189 | Fat: 3 g | Protein: 4 g | Sodium: 312 mg | Fiber: 4 g | Carbohydrates: 26 g | Sugar: 4 g

Southern Potato Salad

Vegenaise is the best vegan mayo option for this classic Southern dish.

INGREDIENTS | SERVES 8

6 potatoes, peeled and cubed

2 stalks celery, chopped

½ cup sweet relish

¾ cup vegan mayonnaise

3 tablespoons mustard

1 teaspoon salt

¼ teaspoon black pepper

1. Add the potatoes to a 4-quart slow cooker and add water to just cover the potatoes. Cover and cook the potatoes on high heat for 4 hours or until tender.

2. Drain the potatoes and allow them to cool completely before continuing.

3. In a large mixing bowl, add the cooled potatoes and remaining ingredients, and stir until just combined. Cover and chill for 2 hours before serving.

PER SERVING | Calories: 218 | Fat: 10 g | Protein: 3.5 g | Sodium: 360 mg | Fiber: 4.5 g | Carbohydrates: 29 g | Sugar: 2 g

Cheesy Peasy Potatoes

Cheese, potatoes, and peas are a classic dinner combo! Use whatever variety of potato you like most, and if you don't like mushrooms, feel free to use cream of celery soup instead.

INGREDIENTS | SERVES 4

8 cups cubed potatoes

1 (14½-ounce) can vegan cream of mushroom soup

3 cups vegan "chicken" broth

2 cups frozen peas

1 cup chopped vegan "bacon"

1 cup shredded vegan Cheddar cheese

1 teaspoon salt

¼ teaspoon black pepper

Add all ingredients to a 4-quart slow cooker. Cover and cook on medium-high heat for 4–5 hours.

PER SERVING | Calories: 504 | Fat: 25 g | Protein: 18 g | Sodium: 1,348 mg | Fiber: 8 g | Carbohydrates: 64 g | Sugar: 9 g

Rosemary Fingerling Potatoes

Fingerling potatoes are small, long potatoes that look a little like fingers.

INGREDIENTS | SERVES 6

2 tablespoons extra-virgin olive oil

1½ pounds fingerling potatoes

1 teaspoon salt

¼ teaspoon black pepper

2 tablespoons chopped, fresh rosemary

1 tablespoon fresh lemon juice

1. Add the olive oil, potatoes, salt, and pepper to a 4-quart slow cooker. Cover and cook on low heat for 3–4 hours.

2. Remove the cover and mix in the rosemary and lemon juice.

PER SERVING | Calories: 121 | Fat: 5 g | Protein: 2 g | Sodium: 401 mg | Fiber: 3.2 g | Carbohydrates: 18.5 g | Sugar: 1 g

Time Saver

To save on time when cooking potatoes, always cut them into the smallest pieces the recipe will allow and cook at the highest temperature. For this recipe, you can quarter the potatoes and cook on high heat.

Dill Red Potatoes

Fresh dill is the perfect herb to season a summer dish. If you can't find it in your supermarket, substitute with 1 tablespoon of dried dill.

INGREDIENTS | SERVES 6

2 tablespoons extra-virgin olive oil

1½ pounds red potatoes

1 teaspoon salt

¼ teaspoon black pepper

2 tablespoons chopped, fresh dill

½ teaspoon lemon pepper

1. Add the olive oil, potatoes, salt, and pepper to a 4-quart slow cooker. Cover and cook on low heat for 3–4 hours.

2. Remove the cover and mix in the dill and lemon pepper.

PER SERVING | Calories: 118 | Fat: 4.6 g | Protein: 2 g | Sodium: 400 mg | Fiber: 2 g | Carbohydrates: 18 g | Sugar: 1 g

Potato Piccata

Piccata typically means a dish that contains butter, lemon, and herbs, but you can veganize it by replacing the butter with Earth Balance. Italian parsley, capers, garlic, and shallots are also commonly used.

INGREDIENTS | SERVES 4

2 tablespoons Earth Balance Original Buttery Spread
1 onion, julienned
1 red pepper, sliced
4 russet potatoes, sliced
¼ cup Vegetable Broth (see Chapter 3)
2 tablespoons fresh lemon juice
1 teaspoon salt
¼ teaspoon black pepper
¼ cup chopped parsley

1. Add the Earth Balance to a 2-quart slow cooker and sauté the onions and peppers on high heat until they are golden brown, about 5–7 minutes.

2. Add the rest of the ingredients except for the parsley. Cover and cook on medium heat for 4 hours. Mix in the parsley.

PER SERVING | Calories: 218 | Fat: 6 g | Protein: 5 g | Sodium: 611 mg | Fiber: 4 g | Carbohydrates: 44 g | Sugar: 4 g

Varieties of Garlic

Most people think of garlic as just "garlic," but there are actually two different subspecies—hard necked and soft necked—and many different varieties. The type most commonly found in grocery stores is artichoke garlic, which is of the soft necked variety.

Herbed Potatoes

Any combination of herbs will work in this potato dish. Rosemary, thyme, dill, and coriander are great alternatives.

INGREDIENTS | SERVES 4

2 tablespoons olive oil
1 onion, diced
8 cups quartered red potatoes
1 teaspoon dried oregano
1 teaspoon dried basil
1 teaspoon salt
¼ teaspoon black pepper

1. Add the olive oil to a 4-quart slow cooker and sauté the onion on high heat until translucent, about 3–5 minutes.

2. Add the remaining ingredients to the slow cooker. Cover and cook on medium heat for 4 hours.

PER SERVING | Calories: 232 | Fat: 7 g | Protein: 5 g | Sodium: 609 mg | Fiber: 5 g | Carbohydrates: 50 g | Sugar: 4 g

Mexican Spice Potatoes

If you like things spicy, really kick it up by adding an extra teaspoon of cayenne to these potatoes!

INGREDIENTS | SERVES 4

6 cups cubed red potatoes
1 teaspoon chili powder
½ teaspoon sugar
½ teaspoon paprika
⅛ teaspoon cayenne pepper
⅛ teaspoon garlic powder
¼ teaspoon cumin
½ teaspoon salt
⅛ teaspoon black pepper
½ cup water

Add all ingredients to a 4-qaurt slow cooker. Cover and cook on high heat for 4 hours.

PER SERVING | Calories: 163 | Fat: 0 g | Protein: 4 g | Sodium: 316 mg | Fiber: 4 g | Carbohydrates: 37 g | Sugar: 3 g

Pot Roast–Style Potatoes

*Add large pieces of chopped seitan to take this dish
from pot roast style to full on veggie pot roast!*

INGREDIENTS | SERVES 6

1 onion, chopped

4 carrots, peeled and chopped

2 stalks celery, chopped

5 cloves garlic

5 medium potatoes, cut into 1-inch cubes

3 cups Vegetable Broth (see Chapter 3)

1 tablespoon vegan Worcestershire sauce

1 teaspoon salt

¼ teaspoon black pepper

Add all ingredients to a 4-quart slow cooker. Cover and cook on low heat for 4–6 hours.

PER SERVING | Calories: 163 | Fat: 0 g | Protein: 4 g | Sodium: 476 mg | Fiber: 6 g | Carbohydrates: 37 g | Sugar: 7 g

Traditional Pot Roast

A more traditional pot roast recipe would contain braised beef that is cooked for a long period of time over low heat. Veggies, such as carrots and potatoes, are typically thrown in the same pot and absorb the cooking liquid, which leads to their delicious flavor and soft texture. Vegan versions recreate the flavor nicely by adding vegan Worcestershire sauce to the broth.

"Baked" Potatoes

This dish is so easy that it takes less than 5 minutes of prep time and is perfect for a busy morning.

INGREDIENTS | SERVES 6

6 medium potatoes, stabbed with a fork

Wrap each potato with tin foil and place in the slow cooker. Cook on low heat for 8–10 hours, or until the potatoes are tender.

PER SERVING | Calories: 146 | Fat: 0 g | Protein: 3.5 g | Sodium: 12 g | Fiber: 5 g | Carbohydrates: 33 g | Sugar: 2.5 g

Ultimate Mashed Potatoes

These are called ultimate potatoes, not because of a long list of fancy ingredients, but because they get the classic combo of margarine, garlic, and milk just right!

INGREDIENTS | SERVES 6

¼ cup Earth Balance Original Buttery Spread

1 small onion, diced

5 cloves garlic, minced

8 medium potatoes, peeled and cut into 1-inch pieces

1½ cups water

½ cup unsweetened soymilk

1 teaspoon salt

¼ teaspoon black pepper

1. Add the Earth Balance, onion, garlic, potatoes, and water to a 4-quart slow cooker. Cover and cook on high heat for 4 hours, or until the potatoes are tender.

2. Add the rest of the ingredients and mash with a potato masher until the desired consistency is reached.

PER SERVING | Calories: 285 | Fat: 8 g | Protein: 6 g | Sodium: 510 mg | Fiber: 7 g | Carbohydrates: 48.5 g | Sugar: 5 g

German Potato Salad

*It's potato salad with a twist! This unique version
has a bold sweet and sour taste, and is served warm.*

INGREDIENTS | SERVES 6

¼ cup olive oil

1 onion, diced

2 tablespoons flour

⅓ cup vinegar

⅓ cup sugar

1 cup water

¼ cup whole-grain mustard

3 pounds red potatoes, cut into ¼-inch slices

1 teaspoon salt

¼ teaspoon black pepper

1. Add the olive oil to a 4-quart slow cooker and sauté the onion on medium-high heat for 5 minutes. Mix in the flour to create a roux, and then add the rest of the ingredients.

2. Cover the slow cooker and cook on high heat for 4 hours, or until the potatoes are tender. Serve warm.

PER SERVING | Calories: 306 | Fat: 10 g | Protein: 5 g | Sodium: 527 mg | Fiber: 4.5 g | Carbohydrates: 51 g | Sugar: 14 g

Potatoes and Leeks

Nothing pairs better with potatoes than the buttery taste of leeks.

INGREDIENTS | SERVES 6

2 tablespoons olive oil

2 leeks, diced

4 potatoes, cut into 1-inch chunks

½ cup Vegetable Broth (see Chapter 3)

½ teaspoon salt

¼ teaspoon black pepper

1. Add the olive oil to a 4-quart slow cooker and sauté the leeks on medium-high heat for 3 minutes.

2. Add the rest of the ingredients to the slow cooker. Cover and cook on high heat for 4 hours, or until the potatoes are tender.

PER SERVING | Calories: 157 | Fat: 5 g | Protein: 3 g | Sodium: 211 mg | Fiber: 4 g | Carbohydrates: 26 g | Sugar: 3 g

In Season

Leeks are in season during the autumn months, but in some parts of the country you can buy them nearly year round. Depending on when you buy them, the flavor and size may differ slightly.

Potato Hot Pot

This dish is a bit labor intensive, but the taste is worth the effort!

INGREDIENTS | SERVES 6

2 tablespoons olive oil

1 onion, diced

1 cup sliced mushrooms

5 cloves garlic, minced

⅛ teaspoon salt

⅛ teaspoon black pepper

¼ cup Earth Balance Original Buttery Spread

¼ cup flour

2 cups plain unsweetened soymilk

¼ cup nutritional yeast

1 tablespoon soy sauce

5 potatoes, peeled and thinly sliced

British Cuisine

Potato hot pots are similar to scalloped potatoes, but this dish hails from England instead of France. One of the main differences between scalloped potatoes and a hot pot is that hot pots can be more like a pie with a potato topping.

1. Add the olive oil to a sauté pan and sauté the onions, mushrooms, and garlic for 5 minutes. Add the salt and pepper to the mixture and set aside.

2. In another small sauce pan, melt the Earth Balance and stir in the flour to make a roux. Slowly add the soymilk until the sauce has thickened, stirring often. Mix in the nutritional yeast and soy sauce and set aside.

3. Grease the bottom of the slow cooker with olive oil and layer the potatoes. Then, pour the onion and mushroom mixture on top of the potatoes. Next, pour the nutritional yeast sauce on top of the mushroom mixture.

4. Cover the slow cooker and cook on low heat for 4 hours, or until the potatoes are tender.

PER SERVING | Calories: 299 | Fat: 10 g | Protein: 10 g | Sodium: 590 mg | Fiber: 5.5 g | Carbohydrates: 37 g | Sugar: 3.5 g

Roasted Garlic Mashed Potatoes

*Not only is roasted garlic delicious, it has also been proven to help
the immune system fight off infectious diseases.*

INGREDIENTS | SERVES 6

8 medium potatoes, cut into 1-inch pieces
2 cups Vegetable Broth (see Chapter 3)
1 head garlic
1 tablespoon olive oil
½ cup unsweetened soymilk
1 teaspoon salt
¼ teaspoon black pepper

1. Add the potatoes and Vegetable Broth to a 4-quart slow cooker and cook on high heat for 4 hours, or until the potatoes are tender. Meanwhile, preheat oven to 350°F, then place the head of garlic in tin foil, drizzle the olive oil over it, and wrap and place in the oven for 1 hour.

2. When the potatoes are tender, add 8–10 roasted garlic cloves and the rest of the ingredients. Mash with a potato masher until the desired consistency is reached.

PER SERVING | Calories: 225 | Fat: 2.5 g | Protein: 5 g | Sodium: 411 mg | Fiber: 6 g | Carbohydrates: 45 g | Sugar: 4 g

Candied Apple and Sweet Potato Salad

*If you're looking to add texture and protein to this salad,
try tossing in a handful of toasted and chopped walnuts.*

INGREDIENTS | SERVES 6

4 sweet potatoes, peeled and cut into 1-inch pieces
2 green apples, peeled and diced
1 cup apple juice
1 teaspoon cinnamon
2 tablespoons brown sugar
½ orange, peel grated
½ lemon, peel grated
½ cup raisins

Add all the ingredients to the slow cooker. Cover and cook on high for 3–4 hours, or until the sweet potatoes are tender.

PER SERVING | Calories: 180 | Fat: 0.2 g | Protein: 2 g | Sodium: 52 mg | Fiber: 4.5 g | Carbohydrates: 45 g | Sugar: 25 g

Scalloped Potatoes

Silken tofu can be used as a substitute for vegan cream cheese if you have difficulty finding the product at your local grocery store.

INGREDIENTS | SERVES 6

2 tablespoons olive oil

1 onion, diced

1 cup sliced mushrooms

5 cloves garlic, minced

8 ounces Tofutti Better Than Cream Cheese

¼ teaspoon salt

¼ teaspoon black pepper

8 red potatoes, peeled and thinly sliced

Which Potato Is Best?

You could practically write a book on how to determine which type of potato is best suited for a particular recipe. To avoid any confusion, remember this general rule: potatoes with a high starch content are better for recipes that call for mashing or whipping potatoes, and a lower starch content is preferred if you want a potato to hold its shape, like in this recipe.

1. Add the olive oil to a sauté pan over medium heat and sauté the onions, mushrooms, and garlic for 5 minutes. Pour the vegetables into a bowl and mix in the cream cheese, salt, and pepper.

2. Grease the bottom of the slow cooker with olive oil and layer it with ⅓ of the potatoes. Spread half of the cream cheese mixture on top of the potatoes. Next, make another layer of potatoes, then another layer of cream cheese mixture, and finally, a last layer of potatoes.

3. Cover the slow cooker and cook on low heat for 4 hours, or until the potatoes are tender.

PER SERVING | Calories: 255 | Fat: 5 g | Protein: 8 g | Sodium: 130 mg | Fiber: 5 g | Carbohydrates: 49 g | Sugar: 4 g

Rice and Grains

Tomatillo Rice

This recipe is similar to jambalaya in that you cook the rice in a tomato-based sauce so the flavors are completely absorbed.

INGREDIENTS | SERVES 4

2 tablespoons olive oil
½ red onion, diced
½ red bell pepper, diced
2 cloves garlic, minced
1 lime, juiced
1 cup tomatillo salsa
1 cup water
1 teaspoon salt
1 cup long-grain white rice
½ cup chopped cilantro

1. Heat the olive oil in a sauté pan over medium heat. Add the onion, bell pepper, and garlic, and sauté about 5 minutes.

2. Transfer to a 4-quart slow cooker. Add all the remaining ingredients except for the cilantro.

3. Cover and cook on high heat for 2½ hours. Check the rice periodically to make sure the liquid hasn't been absorbed too quickly and the rice is not drying out.

4. Stir in the cilantro before serving.

PER SERVING | Calories: 268 | Fat: 7 g | Protein: 5 g | Sodium: 982 mg | Fiber: 3 g | Carbohydrates: 47 g | Sugar: 3 g

Tomatillos

Tomatillos are small green tomatoes that are used in many Latin-inspired dishes. They come with a papery husk that surrounds the edible fruit, which must first be removed. Try to find tomatillos with intact, tight-fitting, light brown husks; if the husk is dry or shriveled, the tomatillo is probably not good.

Wild Mushroom Risotto

This makes a great side dish, but you can also try it as a main course, paired with a green salad.

INGREDIENTS | SERVES 6

1 teaspoon olive oil
1 shallot, minced
2 cloves garlic, minced
8 ounces sliced assorted wild mushrooms
2 cups Arborio rice
2 cups Vegetable Broth (see Chapter 3)
3 cups water
½ teaspoon salt

1. Heat the oil over medium heat in a nonstick pan. Sauté the shallot, garlic, and mushrooms until soft, about 4–5 minutes.

2. Add the rice and ½ cup Vegetable Broth, and cook until the liquid is fully absorbed, about 5 minutes.

3. Scrape the rice mixture into a 4-quart slow cooker. Add the water, salt, and remaining Vegetable Broth.

4. Cover and cook on low for 2 hours. Stir before serving.

PER SERVING | Calories: 272 | Fat: 1.2 g | Protein: 6 g | Sodium: 228 mg | Fiber: 3 g | Carbohydrates: 58 g | Sugar: 2.7 g

Farro and Kale

Farro is a type of wheat that is often used like small pasta or a hearty rice.

INGREDIENTS | SERVES 4

5 cloves garlic, minced
1 tablespoon olive oil
1 cup pearled farro
2 cups kale, chopped
2 cups Vegetable Broth (see Chapter 3)
2 tablespoons red wine vinegar
½ teaspoon salt
¼ teaspoon black pepper

1. In a sauté pan over medium heat, sauté the garlic in the olive oil for 30 seconds to 1 minute. Remove from heat and place in a 4-quart slow cooker.

2. Add all remaining ingredients. Cover and cook on high heat for 2–3 hours.

PER SERVING | Calories: 235 | Fat: 4 g | Protein: 6 g | Sodium: 320 mg | Fiber: 6 g | Carbohydrates: 39 g | Sugar: 1 g

Bulgur with Broccoli and Carrot

This filling and delicious dish makes a comforting meal on a cold day.
Make it complete with a salad or a light soup from Chapter 3.

INGREDIENTS | SERVES 4

2 cups bulgur, uncooked

2 tablespoons Earth Balance Original Buttery Spread

1 cup diced carrots

1 cup chopped broccoli

2 cups Vegetable Broth (see Chapter 3)

1 teaspoon salt

1. Add all ingredients to a 4-quart slow cooker. Cover and cook on low heat for 6 hours.

2. Check the bulgur to see if it is tender, and if not, cook for 1 more hour.

PER SERVING | Calories: 360 | Fat: 6 g | Protein: 9 g | Sodium: 656 mg | Fiber: 10 g | Carbohydrates: 13 g | Sugar: 4.6 g

Bulgur, the World's Oldest Cooked Cereal

Bulgur was being eaten as a warm cooked cereal by Early Neolithic Bulgarians from between 5920 B.C. to 5730 B.C. It is a type of whole-wheat grain that has been cleaned, parboiled, dried, ground into particles, and sifted into size. It is high in fiber, B vitamins, iron, phosphorous, and manganese. Its pleasant nutty flavor makes it not just healthy but delicious, too.

Eggplant "Lasagna"

This no-noodle dish makes for a hearty meal and is perfect served with a light side salad.

INGREDIENTS | SERVES 8

2 (1-pound) eggplants

2 teaspoons olive oil, divided use

1 medium onion, diced

3 cloves garlic, minced

1 tablespoon fresh, minced Italian parsley

1 tablespoon fresh, minced basil

28 ounces canned crushed tomatoes

1 shallot, diced

4 ounces fresh spinach

1 tablespoon dried mixed Italian seasoning

¼ teaspoon salt

½ teaspoon freshly ground black pepper

30 ounces Tofu Ricotta (see recipe in sidebar)

Tofu Ricotta

You can make your own tofu ricotta by crumbling one package of drained tofu, then adding 1 tablespoon lemon juice, 1 teaspoon salt, 1 teaspoon dried parsley, and ½ teaspoon pepper. Or you can use store-bought vegan ricotta.

1. Slice the eggplant lengthwise into ¼-inch thick slices. Set aside.

2. Heat 1 teaspoon olive oil in a nonstick pan over medium heat. Sauté the onion and garlic until just softened, about 1–2 minutes.

3. Add the parsley, basil, and crushed tomatoes. Sauté until the sauce thickens and the liquid has evaporated, about 20 minutes.

4. In a second nonstick pan, heat the remaining oil over medium heat. Sauté the shallot and spinach until the spinach has wilted, about 30 seconds to 1 minute. Drain off any extra liquid.

5. Stir the shallot-spinach mixture, Italian seasoning, salt, and pepper into the Tofu Ricotta. Set aside.

6. Preheat the oven to 375°F. Place the eggplant slices on baking sheets. Bake for 10 minutes. Cool slightly.

   Pour ⅓ of the sauce onto the bottom of a 4-quart slow cooker. Top with a single layer of eggplant. Top with ½ of the cheese mixture. Add ⅓ of the sauce. Top with the rest of the cheese mixture.

8. Layer the remaining eggplant on top, then top with remaining sauce. Cover and cook for 4 hours on low, then cook uncovered for 30 minutes on high.

PER SERVING | Calories: 240 | Fat: 10 g | Protein: 16 g | Sodium: 1,250 mg | Fiber: 5 g | Carbohydrates: 20 g | Sugar: 3 g

Mediterranean Millet

The combination of onion, artichokes, and tomatoes are reminiscent of the Mediterranean in this healthy grain dish.

INGREDIENTS | SERVES 4

¼ cup diced onion

2 tablespoons olive oil

½ cup quartered, marinated artichoke hearts

½ cup diced Roma tomatoes

1 cup millet

2 cups water

1 lemon, juiced

½ teaspoon salt

1. In a sauté pan over medium heat, sauté the onion in the olive oil for 3 minutes. Remove from heat and place in a 4-quart slow cooker.

2. Add all remaining ingredients. Cover and cook on high heat for 1–2 hours, checking to see if the dish is done after 1 hour.

PER SERVING | Calories: 270 | Fat: 9 g | Protein: 7 g | Sodium: 313 mg | Fiber: 6 g | Carbohydrates: 41 g | Sugar: 1.5 g

White Beans and Rice

This one-pot dish is somewhere between a stew and a more traditional entrée, and you can change the consistency to your liking by adding more or less water 1 hour before it's done cooking.

INGREDIENTS | SERVES 8

2 cups dried Great Northern beans

8 cups water

1 white onion, diced

1 carrot, peeled and sliced

2 tablespoons ketchup

1 tablespoon vegan Worcestershire sauce

2 bay leaves

1 teaspoon dried thyme

1 teaspoon salt

½ teaspoon pepper

¾ cup rice

1. Add all ingredients, except for the rice, to a 6- or 8-quart slow cooker. Cover and cook over low heat for 6 hours.

2. Add the rice. Cover and cook on high heat for an additional 2–3 hours, or until the rice is tender.

PER SERVING | Calories: 156 | Fat: 0.3 g | Protein: 6 g | Sodium: 375 mg | Fiber: 4 g | Carbohydrates: 32 g | Sugar: 2 g

Portobello Barley

*This method of cooking barley makes it as creamy as risotto,
but with the bonus of being high in fiber.*

INGREDIENTS | SERVES 8

1 teaspoon olive oil

2 shallots, minced

2 cloves garlic, minced

3 portobello mushroom caps, sliced

1 cup pearl barley

3¼ cups water

¼ teaspoon salt

½ teaspoon freshly ground black pepper

1 teaspoon crushed rosemary

1 teaspoon dried chervil

¼ cup grated vegan Parmesan cheese

Chervil

Chervil is an herb of the parsley family. It has delicate, curly leaves almost like carrot tops. Its mild flavor, which includes hints of anise, is easily overwhelmed by stronger flavors. Fresh parsley, tarragon, or a combination of both can substitute for chervil.

1. Heat the oil in a nonstick skillet over medium heat. Sauté the shallots, garlic, and mushrooms until softened, about 3–4 minutes.

2. Place the mushroom mixture into a 4-quart slow cooker. Add the barley, water, salt, pepper, rosemary, and chervil. Stir.

3. Cover and cook on low for 8–9 hours or on high for 4 hours.

4. Turn off the slow cooker and stir in the vegan Parmesan. Serve immediately.

PER SERVING | Calories: 130 | Fat: 1.5 g | Protein: 5 g | Sodium: 120 mg | Fiber: 5 g | Carbohydrates: 25 g | Sugar: 1 g

Spanish Paella

Paella is a popular yet versatile rice dish that typically includes meat, veggies, and rice in a variety of combinations. So get creative and personalize this dish with your favorite ingredients!

INGREDIENTS | SERVES 6

2 tablespoons olive oil
1 onion, diced
1 bell pepper, seeded and diced
2 cloves garlic, minced
1 cup diced tomato
½ teaspoon saffron or turmeric
1 teaspoon salt
2 tablespoons chopped, fresh parsley
1 cup long-grain white rice
2 cups water
1 (12-ounce) package vegan chorizo, crumbled

1. Heat the olive oil in a sauté pan over medium heat. Add the onion and bell pepper, and sauté for 3 minutes. Add the garlic and sauté for an additional 30 seconds.

2. Pour the sautéed mixture into a 4-quart slow cooker and add all remaining ingredients.

3. Cover and cook on high heat for 2–3 hours, or until the rice is tender.

PER SERVING | Calories: 212 | Fat: 6 g | Protein: 7 g | Sodium: 418 mg | Fiber: 2 g | Carbohydrates: 31 g | Sugar: 2.5 g

Garlic-Pecan Brown Rice

Roasting garlic before using it in recipes brings out a whole new flavor. To enhance this dish even further, try toasting the pecans in a dry skillet for 3–4 minutes before adding to the slow cooker.

INGREDIENTS | SERVES 4

1 head garlic
1 tablespoon olive oil
½ cup finely chopped pecans
1 teaspoon dried parsley
¾ teaspoon salt
2 cups brown rice
3 cups water

1. Preheat the oven to 400°F. Cut the top ¼ off the head of garlic, place in aluminum foil, and drizzle with the olive oil. Seal the aluminum foil at the top (like a small pouch) and cook for 30–45 minutes, or until soft.

2. Allow the garlic to cool completely, then remove each clove from the paper husk.

3. Place all of the roasted garlic and all remaining ingredients in a 4-quart slow cooker. Cover and cook on high heat for 2½–3 hours.

PER SERVING | Calories: 290 | Fat: 6 g | Protein: 7 g | Sodium: 354 mg | Fiber: 3 g | Carbohydrates: 67 g | Sugar: 1 g

Jasmine Rice

*This white rice gets its name from its fragrant, long grains,
and it's most commonly used in Thai cuisine.*

INGREDIENTS | SERVES 8

2 cups jasmine rice

3 cups water

1 teaspoon salt

Combine all ingredients in a 4-quart slow cooker. Cover and cook on high heat for 1 hour, or until rice is tender.

PER SERVING | Calories: 168 | Fat: 0.3 g | Protein: 3.2 g | Sodium: 299 mg | Fiber: 0.5 g | Carbohydrates: 36 g | Sugar: 0 g

To Rinse or Not to Rinse

Many people like to rinse jasmine thoroughly before cooking. To do this, place the rice in a colander and run cold water over the rice until it runs clear. This step isn't crucial, though, so if you're pressed for time, just skip it.

Steamed Rice

Rice is a food staple around the world, especially in China, where it originated.

INGREDIENTS | SERVES 8

2 cups long-grain white rice

4 cups water

Add all ingredients to a 4-quart slow cooker. Cover and cook on high heat for 2–2½ hours. Check to see if rice is done after 2 hours.

PER SERVING | Calories: 179 | Fat: 0 g | Protein: 3 g | Sodium: 4 mg | Fiber: 1.5 g | Carbohydrates: 39 g | Sugar: 0 g

Warm Farro and Herb Salad

*Farro has a nice chewy texture and a flavor similar to barley or spelt,
so you could try using a combination of the grains in this salad.*

INGREDIENTS | SERVES 6

3 cups dried farro

7 cups water

1 teaspoon salt

1 lemon, juiced

1 bunch parsley, chopped

¼ teaspoon black pepper

1. Add the farro, water, and salt to a 4-quart slow cooker and cook on high heat for 2–3 hours, or until the farro is tender and the water absorbed.

2. Stir in the remaining ingredients and serve warm.

PER SERVING | Calories: 288 | Fat: 1 g | Protein: 10 g | Sodium: 390 mg | Fiber: 7 g | Carbohydrates: 60 g | Sugar: 2 g

Time-Saving Tip

If you'd like to save a little time and prepare a grain dish the night before serving, just cover and refrigerate. A few minutes before serving, remove from the fridge, add a little water, and microwave for 2–3 minutes. Adding a small amount of water (up to ¼ cup) will prevent the grains from drying out and will make the dish taste more like it was just prepared.

Two-Grain Cauliflower

If you have the time, enhance this dish by roasting the cauliflower before adding to the slow cooker.

INGREDIENTS | SERVES 6

2 cups cauliflower, small dice

1 cup dried bulgur

1 cup dried quinoa

4 cups water

1 lemon, juiced

½ cup mint, chopped

1 teaspoon salt

¼ teaspoon black pepper

6 teaspoons olive oil

1. Place the cauliflower, bulgur, quinoa, and water in a 4-quart slow cooker. Cook on high heat for 1–2 hours, or until the grains are tender and the water is absorbed.

2. Place the grains in a bowl and allow to cool. Add the lemon juice, mint, salt, and pepper; stir, and drizzle olive oil (1 teaspoon per plate) over each individual plate before serving.

PER SERVING | Calories: 241 | Fat: 6.5 g | Protein: 8 g | Sodium: 320 mg | Fiber: 8 g | Carbohydrates: 39 g | Sugar: 1 g

Basic Brown Rice

Plain and simple is sometimes best, but you can also use this recipe as the base for more creative rice dishes.

INGREDIENTS | SERVES 8

2 cups brown rice

3 cups water

Add all ingredients to a 4-quart slow cooker. Cover and cook on high heat for 2½–3 hours. Check to see if rice is done after 2½ hours.

PER SERVING | Calories: 171 | Fat: 1 g | Protein: 3.5 g | Sodium: 4 mg | Fiber: 1.5 g | Carbohydrates: 36 g | Sugar: 0 g

CHAPTER 10

Beans

Open-Faced Bean Burrito

*Salsas come in many different flavors depending on which ingredients are used,
but any type of salsa (except fruit-based salsa) will work in this recipe.*

INGREDIENTS | SERVES 8

1 (16-ounce) bag dried black beans
Water, enough to cover beans by 1-inch
4 teaspoons salt, divided
1 tablespoon chili powder
2 teaspoons cumin
2 teaspoons garlic powder
1 teaspoon black pepper
1 (15-ounce) can corn, drained
2 fresh tomatoes, diced
8 large flour tortillas
4 cups cooked brown rice
2 cups shredded vegan Cheddar cheese
2 cups salsa
¼ cup chopped cilantro

Alternate Suggestions

Burrito fillings can easily be used in other dishes. Try the beans, rice, and toppings over a bed of lettuce for a taco salad, in soft corn tortillas for delicious tacos, or as a hearty meal on their own.

1. Rinse the black beans, then soak overnight.

2. Drain the beans, rinse again, then add to a large pot and cover with water. Boil on high heat for 10 minutes and drain.

3. Add black beans, water, and 2 teaspoons salt to a 4-qaurt slow cooker. Cover and cook on medium heat for about 5–6 hours. Check the beans at about 5 hours to see if they are fork-tender. Continue cooking if necessary.

4. Once the beans are done, drain in a colander and allow to cool to room temperature.

5. In a large bowl, mix in with the beans the remaining salt, chili powder, cumin, garlic powder, black pepper, corn, and tomatoes.

6. Place a tortilla on a plate. Add a scoop of the brown rice and then a scoop of the black bean mixture. Top with the vegan cheese, salsa, and cilantro, if desired.

PER SERVING | Calories: 798 | Fat: 18 g | Protein: 27 g | Sodium: 2,629 mg | Fiber: 12 g | Carbohydrates: 120 g | Sugar: 6 g

White Beans with Rosemary and Fresh Tomato

Rosemary is a cheap and easy herb to maintain in your garden.

INGREDIENTS | SERVES 8

2 (15-ounce) cans white beans, drained

1 cup water

1 teaspoon salt

3 tablespoons extra-virgin olive oil

4 cloves garlic, minced

2 cups diced tomatoes

3 tablespoons chopped, fresh rosemary

¼ teaspoon black pepper

Add all ingredients to a 4-quart slow cooker. Cover and cook on low heat for about 5–6 hours.

PER SERVING | Calories: 143 | Fat: 5.5 g | Protein: 6 g | Sodium: 509 mg | Fiber: 6 g | Carbohydrates: 17 g | Sugar: 3 g

Mediterranean Chickpeas

Chickpeas, also known as garbanzo beans, are the main ingredient in this delicious dish that can be served hot or cold.

INGREDIENTS | SERVES 8

2 (15-ounce) cans chickpeas, drained

1 cup water

4 teaspoons salt

¼ cup extra-virgin olive oil

1 teaspoon black pepper

1 cup chopped, fresh basil

5 cloves garlic, minced

2 tomatoes, diced

½ cup sliced kalamata olives

Add all ingredients to a 4-quart slow cooker. Cover and cook on low heat for 4 hours.

PER SERVING | Calories: 243 | Fat: 8 g | Protein: 7 g | Sodium: 1,208 mg | Fiber: 6 g | Carbohydrates: 37 g | Sugar: 3 g

Curried Lentils

Serve this Indian-style dish with hot rice or naan, an Indian flatbread.
It can also be served with vegan yogurt as garnish or on the side.

INGREDIENTS | SERVES 6

2 teaspoons canola oil

1 large onion, thinly sliced

2 cloves garlic, minced

2 jalapeños, diced

½ teaspoon red pepper flakes

½ teaspoon ground cumin

1 pound yellow lentils

6 cups water

½ teaspoon salt

½ teaspoon ground turmeric

4 cups chopped, fresh spinach

1. Heat the oil in a nonstick pan over medium heat. Sauté the onion slices until they start to brown, about 8–10 minutes.

2. Add the garlic, jalapeños, red pepper flakes, and cumin. Sauté for 2–3 minutes.

3. Add the onion mixture to a 4-quart slow cooker.

4. Sort through the lentils and discard any rocks or foreign matter. Add the lentils to the slow cooker. Stir in the water, salt, and turmeric.

5. Cover and cook on high for 2½ hours.

6. Add the spinach and stir. Cook on high for an additional 15 minutes.

PER SERVING | Calories: 280 | Fat: 2 g | Protein: 21 g | Sodium: 210 mg | Fiber: 10 g | Carbohydrates: 49 g | Sugar: 2.5 g

Hoppin' John

In the South, black-eyed peas are often cooked with meat, such as ham, to flavor the beans, but in this vegan version the liquid smoke replaces the meaty flavor.

INGREDIENTS | SERVES 8

1 cup dried black-eyed peas, rehydrated

¾ cup water

1 teaspoon liquid smoke

1 teaspoon red pepper flakes

3 cups diced mustard or collard greens

14 ounces canned tomatoes

½ teaspoon freshly ground black pepper

¼ teaspoon salt

1 teaspoon dried oregano

1. Place all ingredients into a 4-quart slow cooker. Stir.

2. Cover and cook on high for 5 hours.

PER SERVING | Calories: 80 g | Fat: 0.5 g | Protein: 5 g | Sodium: 220 mg | Fiber: 6 g | Carbohydrates: 12 g | Sugar: 2.5 g

Quick Prep for Black-Eyed Peas

Here's a method to quickly and easily prepare black-eyed peas: place the peas in a large stockpot, cover completely with water, and bring to a boil. Boil 2 minutes, reduce heat, and simmer for 1 hour.

Bourbon Baked Beans

Serve these at your next cookout or as a side dish for BBQ tempeh or tofu.

INGREDIENTS | SERVES 8

1 large sweet onion, peeled and diced

3 (15-ounce) cans cannellini, Great Northern, or navy beans

1 (15-ounce) can diced tomatoes

¼ cup maple syrup

3 tablespoons apple cider vinegar

1 teaspoon liquid smoke

4 cloves garlic, peeled and minced

2 tablespoons dry mustard

1½ teaspoons freshly ground black pepper

½ teaspoon ground ginger

¼ teaspoon dried red pepper flakes

2 tablespoons bourbon

¼ teaspoon salt (optional)

1. Add all ingredients to a 4-quart slow cooker. Stir until combined.

2. Cover and cook on low heat for 6 hours. Taste for seasoning and add salt if needed.

PER SERVING | Calories: 290 | Fat: 2 g | Protein: 15 g | Sodium: 130 mg | Fiber: 9 g | Carbohydrates: 48 g | Sugar: 9 g

Recipe Variations

Some bourbon baked bean recipes include much more tomato than this one. If you prefer more tomato, you can add 1 (4-ounce) can tomato paste or about 2 tablespoons ketchup when you stir in all of the other ingredients.

Cannellini Beans in Tomato Broth

*Adding a little salt while cooking will help bring out the flavor
of the beans, but this ingredient is optional.*

INGREDIENTS | SERVES 8

1 (16-ounce) bag dried cannellini beans

Enough water to cover beans by 1 inch

3 cups water

2 cups Vegetable Broth (see Chapter 3)

1 (14-ounce) can fire-roasted tomatoes

2 cloves garlic, minced

1 sprig fresh thyme

2 bay leaves

1 teaspoon salt

Bay Leaf

Bay leaves are often used to season soups and stews, but before adding them, crumble the leaf in order to extract the most flavor. To crumble the leaves, it's best to place them in an herb bag or cheesecloth so that you can easily remove them after cooking.

1. Rinse the cannellini beans, then soak overnight. Drain the water and rinse the beans again.

2. In a large pot, add the beans and cover with water. Boil on high heat for 10 minutes, then drain.

3. Add beans, water, Vegetable Broth, fire-roasted tomatoes, garlic, thyme, bay leaves, and salt to a 4-quart slow cooker. Cover and cook on medium heat for about 5–6 hours. Check the beans at about 5 hours to see if they are tender, and continue cooking if necessary.

4. Once the beans are done, remove the bay leaves and serve in the broth.

PER SERVING | Calories: 198 | Fat: 0.5 g | Protein: 13.5 g | Sodium: 352 mg | Fiber: 9 g | Carbohydrates: 36 g | Sugar: 2.5 g

Mexican Beer Black Beans

Try a Mexican beer such as Negra Modelo, Tecate, or Corona to complement the beans in this recipe.

INGREDIENTS | SERVES 8

1 (16-ounce) bag dried black beans
Enough water to cover beans by ½ inch
2 (12-ounce) bottles light-colored beer
4 teaspoons salt, divided
1 red onion, diced
4 cloves garlic, minced
2 fresh tomatoes, diced
½ cup chopped cilantro
1 lime, juiced

1. Rinse the black beans, then soak overnight. Drain the water and then rinse the beans again.

2. Add the beans to a large pot and cover with water. Boil on high heat for 10 minutes, then drain.

3. Add black beans, water, beer, and 2 teaspoons salt to a 4-quart slow cooker. Cover, and cook on medium heat for about 5–6 hours. Check the beans at about 5 hours to see if they are tender and continue cooking if necessary.

4. Once the beans are done, drain in a colander.

5. In a large bowl, combine the beans, remaining salt, red onions, garlic, tomatoes, cilantro, and lime.

PER SERVING | Calories: 243 | Fat: 0.9 g | Protein: 13 g | Sodium: 1,188 mg | Fiber: 7 g | Carbohydrates: 42 g | Sugar: 2.7 g

Lentils with Sautéed Spinach, White Wine, and Garlic

Keep a close eye on this one, as spinach takes only a few seconds to sauté perfectly.

INGREDIENTS | SERVES 8

1 (16-ounce) bag dried lentils

Enough water to cover lentils by 1 inch

2 teaspoons salt

2 tablespoons olive oil

8 cups packed fresh spinach

5 cloves garlic, minced

⅛ cup tablespoons white wine

1 teaspoon black pepper

Which Wine?

When cooking with white wine, avoid using a wine that is overly fruity or floral, like a riesling. Good options for cooking wines include chardonnay and sauvignon blanc.

1. Add lentils, water, and 1 teaspoon of salt to a 4-quart slow cooker. Cover and cook on medium heat for about 3–4 hours. Check the lentils at about 4 hours, and continue cooking if necessary.

2. Once the lentils are done, drain in a colander and allow them to cool to room temperature.

3. While the lentils are cooling, add the olive oil to a large pan and sauté the spinach with the garlic and white wine over medium-low heat for 3–5 minutes.

4. In a large bowl, combine the lentils with the sautéed spinach and the remaining salt and pepper.

PER SERVING | Calories: 232 | Fat: 4 g | Protein: 15 g | Sodium: 602 mg | Fiber: 7 g | Carbohydrates: 35 g | Sugar: 1 g

Chana Masala

The main ingredient in the popular Indian dish chana masala is chickpeas.

INGREDIENTS | SERVES 8

2 (15-ounce) cans chickpeas, drained

1 cup water

4 teaspoons salt

¼ cup Earth Balance Original Buttery Spread

1 onion, diced

5 cloves garlic, minced

1 tablespoon cumin

½ teaspoon cayenne pepper

1 teaspoon ground turmeric

2 teaspoons paprika

1 teaspoon garam masala

1 cup diced tomatoes

1 lemon, juiced

2 teaspoons grated ginger

Add all ingredients to a 4-quart slow cooker. Cover and cook on low heat for 6 hours.

PER SERVING | Calories: 208 | Fat: 7 g | Protein: 7 g | Sodium: 1,210 mg | Fiber: 5 g | Carbohydrates: 30 g | Sugar: 2 g

Indian Cuisine

Due to the size of India and its abundance of spices, Indian cuisine varies by region, community, and religion, but they are all similar. Herbs and spices such as coriander, curry powder, and garam masala are commonly used as well as rice and a variety of lentils.

Summer Vegetable Bean Salad

Serve this salad warm, straight out of the slow cooker, or chilled and over a bed of lettuce.

INGREDIENTS | SERVES 8

1 (15-ounce) can black beans

1 (15-ounce) can red kidney beans

1 (15-ounce) can white beans

1 cup water

1 red onion, diced

1 green bell pepper, diced

1 red bell pepper, diced

¼ cup chopped cilantro

½ cup red wine vinegar

½ cup extra-virgin olive oil

1 teaspoon black pepper

Add all ingredients to a 4-quart slow cooker. Cover and cook on low heat for 4 hours.

PER SERVING | Calories: 400 | Fat: 14 g | Protein: 17 g | Sodium: 321 mg | Fiber: 14 g | Carbohydrates: 50 g | Sugar: 4.5 g

White Beans

Great Northern beans, navy beans, and cannellini beans are all referred to as white beans, but each has its own unique qualities. Cannellini beans work best if you want the bean to hold its shape and texture after a long cooking time.

Spicy Black-Eyed Peas and Kale

Black-eyed peas are a good source of fiber, protein, and iron.

INGREDIENTS | SERVES 8

1 (16-ounce) bag dried black-eyed peas
Enough water to cover black-eyed peas by 1 inch
2 teaspoons salt
2 tablespoons olive oil
1 onion, diced
5 cloves garlic, minced
1 pound kale, chopped
½ teaspoon cayenne pepper
2 teaspoons cumin
1 teaspoon black pepper

1. Rinse the black-eyed peas, then soak overnight. Drain the water and rinse the peas again.

2. In a large pot, add the peas and cover with water. Boil on high heat for 10 minutes, then drain.

3. Add black-eyed peas, water, and salt to a 4-quart slow cooker. Cover and cook on medium heat for about 5–6 hours. Check the black-eyed peas at about 5 hours, and continue cooking if necessary.

4. Once the black-eyed peas are done, drain in a colander.

5. Add the olive oil to the slow cooker set on high heat and sauté the onion, garlic, and kale for about 5 minutes.

6. Add the rest of the ingredients, including the black-eyed peas, to the slow cooker. Cover and allow to cook for 15–20 minutes more.

PER SERVING | Calories: 256 | Fat: 4.5 g | Protein: 15 g | Sodium: 524 mg | Fiber: 7.5 g | Carbohydrates: 41 g | Sugar: 4 g

Chipotle Black Bean Salad

There are actually five different varieties of black beans, but when you purchase them at the grocery store, they are often just labeled as "black beans."

INGREDIENTS | SERVES 8

1 (16-ounce) bag dried black beans
Enough water to cover beans by 1 inch
2 teaspoons salt
1 tablespoon chipotle powder
2 teaspoons thyme
2 fresh tomatoes, diced
1 red onion, diced
¼ cup chopped cilantro

Prepping Dried Beans

Before cooking with dried beans, you must first rinse the beans, soak them overnight in a pot full of water, and then boil them for 10 minutes. They are then ready for step 1 of the recipe.

1. Add black beans, water, and salt to a 4-quart slow cooker. Cover and cook on medium heat for about 5–6 hours. Check the beans at about 5 hours to see if they are tender and continue cooking if necessary.

2. Once the beans are done, drain in a colander and allow to cool to room temperature.

3. Mix in the remaining ingredients and serve.

PER SERVING | Calories: 198 | Fat: 1 g | Protein: 10 g | Sodium: 768 mg | Fiber: 7 g | Carbohydrates: 37 g | Sugar: 2.5 g

Edamame Seaweed Salad

Fresh edamame can be very hard to find in the United States,
so using frozen beans instead might be your only option.

INGREDIENTS | SERVES 4

1 (10-ounce) package frozen shelled edamame

Water, enough to cover edamame by 1 inch

½ cup chopped seaweed

2 cloves garlic, minced

1 teaspoon minced, fresh ginger

1 teaspoon rice wine vinegar

½ teaspoon salt

1 tablespoon soy sauce

2 teaspoons sesame seeds

1. Add edamame, water, seaweed, garlic, and ginger to a 4-qaurt slow cooker. Cover and cook on high heat for about 1–2 hours. Check the edamame after 1 hour and continue cooking if necessary.

2. Once the edamame is done, drain in a colander and allow to cool in a bowl. When the edamame salad is cold, add the rice wine vinegar, salt, soy sauce, and sesame seeds.

PER SERVING | Calories: 120 | Fat: 5.5 g | Protein: 10 g | Sodium: 453 mg | Fiber: 3 g | Carbohydrates: 10 g | Sugar: 0 g

Tri-Color Lentils

Using multiple types of lentils leads to a colorful and festive dish.
This batch of lentils is seasoned very simply, so feel free to spice it up as you wish.

INGREDIENTS | SERVES 8

1 cup red lentils

1 cup green lentils

1 cup yellow lentils

Water, enough to cover lentils by 1 inch

2 teaspoons salt

1. Add lentils, water, and salt to a 4-quart slow cooker, cover, and cook on medium heat for about 3–4 hours. Check the lentils at about 3½ hours and continue cooking if necessary.

2. Once the lentils are done, drain in a colander.

3. Try serving over a small bed of rice or as a simple side dish.

PER SERVING | Calories: 180 | Fat: 1 g | Protein: 13 g | Sodium: 493 mg | Fiber: 6 g | Carbohydrates: 31 g | Sugar: 1 g

Sesame Adzuki Beans

Adzuki beans are Asian beans that are typically enjoyed sweetened, but they can be served savory, too.

INGREDIENTS | SERVES 8

1 (16-ounce) bag dried adzuki beans

Water, enough to cover beans by 1 inch

1 teaspoon salt

1 tablespoon sesame oil

1 tablespoon soy sauce

1 teaspoon rice wine vinegar

2 teaspoons toasted sesame seeds

1. Add the adzuki beans, water, and salt to a 4-quart slow cooker. Cover and cook on medium heat for about 5–6 hours. Check the beans at about 5 hours to see if they are tender and continue cooking if necessary.

2. Once the beans are done, drain in a colander and allow to cool.

3. Pour the beans into a bowl and stir in the sesame oil, soy sauce, rice wine vinegar, and sesame seeds.

PER SERVING | Calories: 204 | Fat: 2 g | Protein: 11 g | Sodium: 390 mg | Fiber: 7 g | Carbohydrates: 35 g | Sugar: 0 g

Chipotle Pinto Beans

For an even spicier version of this recipe, add a ½ teaspoon of cayenne pepper (or more!) with the other spices.

INGREDIENTS | SERVES 8

1 (16-ounce) bag dried pinto beans

Water, enough to cover beans by 1 inch

1 teaspoon salt

2 teaspoons chipotle chili powder

1 teaspoon dried thyme

Add all ingredients to a 4-quart slow cooker. Cover and cook on medium heat for about 5–6 hours. Check the beans at about 5 hours to see if they are tender and continue cooking if necessary.

PER SERVING | Calories: 194 | Fat: 0.5 g | Protein: 12 g | Sodium: 301 mg | Fiber: 8.5 g | Carbohydrates: 35 g | Sugar: 1 g

Creole Red Beans

Creole-style red beans are traditionally served over a heaping bowl of steamed white rice.

INGREDIENTS | SERVES 8

1 (16-ounce) bag dried red kidney beans
Water, enough to cover beans by 1 inch
2 teaspoons salt
1 tablespoon Cajun seasoning
2 teaspoons liquid smoke
1 teaspoon vegan Worcestershire sauce
2 teaspoons hot sauce
1 teaspoon dried thyme
2 teaspoons cayenne pepper
4 bay leaves

1. Add all ingredients to a 4-quart slow cooker. Cover and cook on medium heat for about 5–6 hours. Check the beans at about 5 hours to see if they are tender and continue cooking if necessary.

2. Serve warm over a bed of rice.

PER SERVING | Calories: 191 | Fat: 0.5 g | Protein: 12 g | Sodium: 534 mg | Fiber: 8.5 g | Carbohydrates: 34 g | Sugar: 1 g

Liquid Smoke

Liquid smoke, which is found in the condiment aisle, is an easy way to add a smoky, hearty flavor to any dish. The concentrated liquid is made by condensing smoke (usually from burning hickory wood) to a liquid, or by channeling water through the smoke to pick up the smoky flavor. Some producers add additional flavoring such as vinegar and molasses.

Drunken Refried Beans

If you don't have a potato masher for this recipe, use a food processor or blender.

INGREDIENTS | **SERVES 8**

1 (16-ounce) bag dried pinto beans

Water, enough to cover beans by 1 inch

2 (12-ounce) bottles light-colored beer

2 teaspoons salt, divided

4 cloves garlic, minced

1. Add pinto beans, water, beer, and 1 teaspoon salt to a 4-quart slow cooker. Cover and cook on medium heat for about 5–6 hours. Check the beans at about 5 hours to see if they are tender and continue cooking if necessary.

2. Once the beans are done, drain in a colander, reserving about 1 cup of the cooking liquid. In a large bowl, combine the beans, remaining salt, and garlic. Mash the bean mixture with a potato masher, adding reserved cooking liquid as needed until a smooth consistency is reached.

PER SERVING | Calories: 232 | Fat: 0.5 g | Protein: 12 g | Sodium: 499 mg | Fiber: 8.5 g | Carbohydrates: 38 g | Sugar: 1 g

Mexican Black Bean Casserole

Enjoy this dish on its own or as a festive dip.

INGREDIENTS | SERVES 8

2 (15-ounce) cans black beans, drained

1 red onion, diced

1 cup corn kernels

2 cloves garlic, minced

2 fresh Roma tomatoes, diced

½ cup cilantro

1 lime, juiced

1 cup vegan Cheddar cheese

2 cups crumbled tortilla chips, divided

1. Add black beans, onion, corn, garlic, tomatoes, cilantro, lime juice, vegan cheese, and 1 cup tortilla chips to a 4-quart slow cooker and stir well.

2. Top with the remaining tortilla chips. Cover and cook on low heat for 3 hours.

PER SERVING | Calories: 245 | Fat: 9 g | Protein: 11 g | Sodium: 452 mg | Fiber: 7 g | Carbohydrates: 30 g | Sugar: 4 g

Garlic and Sage Borlotti Beans

*If you can't find borlotti beans at your local grocery store,
cannellini beans make a good substitute.*

INGREDIENTS | SERVES 8

1 (16-ounce) bag dried borlotti beans

Water, enough to cover beans by 1 inch

2 teaspoons salt

2 tablespoons extra-virgin olive oil

4 cloves garlic, minced

2 cups diced tomatoes

1 teaspoon dried sage

¼ teaspoon black pepper

Add all of the ingredients to a 4-quart slow cooker. Cover and cook on medium heat for about 5–6 hours. Check the beans at about 5 hours to see if they are tender and continue cooking if necessary. Serve as a side dish.

PER SERVING | Calories: 227 | Fat: 4 g | Protein: 13 g | Sodium: 495 mg | Fiber: 14 g | Carbohydrates: 35 g | Sugar: 1 g

Borlotti Beans

Borlotti beans are commonly used in Italian and Greek cuisine and can be identified by their white skin and red speckles. They have a thick, meaty flavor and hold up well to heavy seasonings like garlic and dried sage.

Fresh Fava Bean Salad

*The fava bean is native to northern Africa and southwest Asia,
and it is easy to find at grocery stores in the United States.*

INGREDIENTS | SERVES 10

1 (16-ounce) bag dried fava beans

Water, enough to cover beans by 1 inch

2 teaspoons salt, divided

2 tablespoons extra-virgin olive oil

2 cups diced tomatoes

2 cloves garlic

1 cucumber, seeded and chopped

3 tablespoons chopped, fresh parsley

1 lemon, juiced

1 teaspoon paprika

¼ teaspoon black pepper

1. Add the fava beans, water, and 1 teaspoon salt to a 4-quart slow cooker. Cover and cook on medium heat for about 5–6 hours. Check the beans at about 5 hours to see if they are tender and continue cooking if necessary.

2. Once the beans are done, drain in a colander and allow to cool to room temperature.

3. In a large bowl, combine the beans with the remaining ingredients and refrigerate for at least 2 hours before serving.

PER SERVING | Calories: 191 | Fat: 3.5 g | Protein: 12 g | Sodium: 410 mg | Fiber: 12 g | Carbohydrates: 29 g | Sugar: 4 g

Lima Bean and Tomato Salad

*This salad is delicious straight out of the slow cooker,
or it can be chilled for 2 hours and served on a cold bed of greens.*

INGREDIENTS | SERVES 4

2 cups frozen lima beans

1 red bell pepper, seeded and diced

½ red onion, chopped

3 Roma tomatoes, diced

1 cup Vegetable Broth (see Chapter 3)

1 tablespoon extra-virgin olive oil

2 tablespoons chopped, fresh parsley

½ teaspoon salt

¼ teaspoon black pepper

Add all ingredients to a 4-quart slow cooker. Cover and cook on low heat for 3–4 hours.

PER SERVING | Calories: 151 | Fat: 4 g | Protein: 7 g | Sodium: 302 mg | Fiber: 7 g | Carbohydrates: 23 g | Sugar: 5 g

Proper Cooling

It's important to cool food properly so that you will prevent the growth of dangerous bacteria. For this recipe, and all solid foods, it's recommended that you quickly place the salad in a shallow dish and into the refrigerator so the temperature can drop quickly.

CHAPTER 11

Tofu

Ginger-Lime Tofu

*The slow cooker does all the work in this recipe, creating a healthy
yet impressive dish that requires virtually no hands-on time.*

INGREDIENTS | SERVES 8

2 (14-ounce) packages extra-firm tofu,
pressed and sliced into fourths

¼ cup minced fresh ginger

¼ cup lime juice

1 lime, thinly sliced

1 onion, thinly sliced

Cracked!

Before each use, check your slow cooker
for cracks. Even small cracks in the glaze
can allow bacteria to grow in the ceramic
insert. If there are cracks, replace the insert
or the whole slow cooker.

1. Place the tofu fillets in an oval 6- to 7-quart slow
   cooker. Pour the ginger and lime juice over the tofu,
   then arrange the lime and then the onion in a single
   layer over the top.

2. Cook on low for 3–4 hours.

PER SERVING | Calories: 75 | Fat: 2 g | Protein: 8 g |
Sodium: 63 mg | Fiber: 1 g | Carbohydrates: 6 g | Sugar: 1.8 g

Tofu with Lemon, Capers, and Rosemary

For an even bolder flavor, try marinating the tofu overnight before cooking.

INGREDIENTS | SERVES 4

1 (14-ounce) package extra-firm tofu, pressed and sliced into quarters

⅓ cup water

2 tablespoons lemon juice

½ teaspoon salt

3 thin slices fresh lemon

1 tablespoon nonpareil capers

½ teaspoon minced fresh rosemary

1. Place the tofu fillets on the bottom of a 2-quart slow cooker. Pour the water, lemon juice, and salt over the tofu.

2. Arrange the lemon slices in a single layer on top of the tofu. Sprinkle with capers and rosemary.

3. Cover and cook on low for 2 hours. Discard lemon slices prior to serving.

PER SERVING | Calories: 57 | Fat: 2 g | Protein: 7 g | Sodium: 412 mg | Fiber: 0.3 g | Carbohydrates: 3 g | Sugar: 1 g

General Tso's Tofu

The combination of sweet and spicy is what makes this dish a hit at Chinese restaurants across the country.

INGREDIENTS | SERVES 2

1 (14-ounce) package of extra-firm tofu, pressed and cubed

1 cup water

2 tablespoons cornstarch

2 cloves garlic, minced

1 teaspoon minced ginger

2 tablespoons sugar

2 tablespoons soy sauce

2 tablespoons white wine vinegar

2 tablespoons sherry

2 teaspoons cayenne pepper

2 tablespoons vegetable oil

2 cups chopped broccoli

Add all ingredients to a 4-quart slow cooker. Cover and cook on medium heat for 4 hours.

PER SERVING | Calories: 75 | Fat: 2 g | Protein: 8 g | Sodium: 63 mg | Fiber: 1 g | Carbohydrates: 6 g | Sugar: 1.8 g

Blackened Tofu

*Preparing blackened tofu on the grill is a delicious alternative
to using a slow cooker on a warm summer day.*

INGREDIENTS | SERVES 4

2 (14-ounce) packages extra-firm tofu,
pressed and quartered

⅓ cup soy sauce

1 tablespoon apple cider vinegar

1 tablespoon minced garlic

1 tablespoon paprika

2 teaspoons black pepper

1½ teaspoons salt

1 teaspoon garlic powder

1 teaspoon cayenne pepper

½ teaspoon dried oregano

½ teaspoon dried thyme

2 tablespoons vegetable oil

1. Place the tofu, soy sauce, vinegar, and garlic in a small bowl and allow to marinate for 10 minutes.

2. To make the blackened seasoning mixture, combine the paprika, black pepper, salt, garlic powder, cayenne, oregano, and thyme in a small bowl. Remove the tofu from the soy marinade and dip each side into the blackened seasoning.

3. Add the oil and blackened tofu to the 2-quart slow cooker. Cover and cook on low heat for 4 hours.

PER SERVING | Calories: 195 | Fat: 10 g | Protein: 16.5 g | Sodium: 1,207 mg | Fiber: 1.5 g | Carbohydrates: 9 g | Sugar: 2.5 g

Types of Tofu

Most major grocery stores carry two different types of tofu—regular or silken. Regular tofu is what you should always use unless the recipe specifically calls for silken, which is most common in desserts or recipes where the tofu needs a creamy consistency.

Mock Meatloaf

*Crumbled tofu, veggie beef crumbles, or textured vegetable protein
will work as the base for this recipe.*

INGREDIENTS | SERVES 4

2 (14-ounce) packages extra-firm tofu, pressed and crumbled

¼ cup oats

¼ cup panko bread crumbs

½ cup ketchup, divided

1 teaspoon garlic powder

2 teaspoons vegan Worcestershire sauce, divided

½ onion, diced

3 garlic cloves, minced

½ jalapeño, minced

½ teaspoon black pepper

1 tablespoon brown sugar

2 teaspoons mustard

1. In a large bowl, combine the tofu, oats, bread crumbs, 3 tablespoons ketchup, garlic powder, 1 teaspoon Worcestershire sauce, onion, garlic, jalapeno, and black pepper.

2. Press the mixture into the base of 2-quart slow cooker that has been prepped with cooking spray. Cover and cook on low heat for 4–6 hours.

3. In a small bowl, combine the remaining ketchup and Worcestershire sauce, brown sugar, and mustard. Pour the sauce on top of the "meatloaf" and continue cooking for 20 more minutes.

PER SERVING | Calories: 212 | Fat: 4.5 g | Protein: 17 g | Sodium: 467 mg | Fiber: 1.5 g | Carbohydrates: 26 g | Sugar: 13 g

Palak Tofu

Palak tofu is a fresh-tasting, protein-rich Indian dish that is only slightly spicy.

INGREDIENTS | SERVES 4

1 (14-ounce) package extra-firm tofu
1 tablespoon canola oil
1 teaspoon cumin seeds
2 cloves garlic, minced
2 jalapeños, minced
¾ pound red skin potatoes, diced
½ teaspoon ground ginger
¾ teaspoon garam masala
1 pound frozen cut-leaf spinach
¼ cup fresh cilantro

Serving Suggestions

There are many different ways to enjoy Indian dishes such as this one. Try it over a bed of Jasmine Rice (see Chapter 9), scoop it up with naan (Indian flatbread), or roll it up in chapatti (another type of flatbread).

1. Cut the tofu into ½-inch cubes. Set aside.

2. Heat the oil in a nonstick skillet. Add the cumin seeds and sauté for 1 minute.

3. Add the garlic and jalapeños. Sauté until fragrant, about 1 minute.

4. Add the tofu and potatoes. Sauté for 3 minutes.

5. Add the ginger, garam masala, frozen spinach, and cilantro. Sauté 1 minute.

6. Pour the mixture into a 4-quart slow cooker and cook for 4 hours on low.

PER SERVING | Calories: 190 | Fat: 7 g | Protein: 14 g | Sodium: 150 mg | Fiber: 5 g | Carbohydrates: 22 g | Sugar: 3 g

Thai Tofu Coconut Curry

Try this easy curry tossed with rice noodles or over brown rice.

INGREDIENTS | SERVES 6

12 ounces extra-firm tofu
¼ cup unsweetened shredded coconut
¼ cup water
4 cloves garlic, minced
1 tablespoon minced, fresh ginger
1 tablespoon minced galangal root
½ cup chopped onion
1 cup peeled and diced sweet potato
1 cup broccoli florets
1 cup snow peas
3 tablespoons tamari
1 tablespoon vegetarian fish sauce
1 tablespoon chili-garlic sauce
½ cup minced, fresh cilantro
½ cup light coconut milk

1. Slice the tofu into ½-inch thick triangles.

2. Place the tofu into a 4-quart slow cooker. Top with coconut, water, garlic, ginger, galangal, onion, sweet potato, broccoli, snow peas, tamari, vegetarian fish sauce, and chili-garlic sauce.

3. Stir to distribute all ingredients evenly. Cook on low for 5 hours.

4. Stir in the cilantro and coconut milk. Cook on low for an additional 20 minutes. Stir prior to serving.

PER SERVING | Calories: 140 | Fat: 8 g | Protein: 7 g | Sodium: 670 mg | Fiber: 3 g | Carbohydrates: 13 g | Sugar: 3 g

Vegetarian Fish Sauce

Vegetarian fish sauce can be found in some Asian markets or online stores such as VeryAsia.com (*www.veryasia.com*). Ingredients vary, but it usually contains soybeans, salt, sugar, water, and chili with citric acid for a preservative since it's not fermented.

Panang Tofu

Panang is a red curry that is often milder than other curries,
but if you'd like to spice it up, you can add extra peppers.

INGREDIENTS | SERVES 2

1 (14-ounce) package extra-firm tofu, pressed and cubed

1 (13-ounce) can coconut milk

1 tablespoon Panang curry paste

2 tablespoons soy sauce

1 tablespoon lime juice

2 tablespoons sugar

2 tablespoons olive oil

¼ onion, sliced

½ carrot, sliced diagonally

½ red bell pepper, chopped

½ cup chopped, fresh basil

1. Add all ingredients except for the basil to a 4-quart slow cooker. Cover and cook on low heat for 4–6 hours.

2. Add the basil before serving.

PER SERVING | Calories: 667 | Fat: 56 g | Protein: 20 g | Sodium: 1,213 mg | Fiber: 2 g | Carbohydrates: 28 g | Sugar: 17.5 g

Barbecue Tofu

Serve this barbecue tofu with a side of baked beans and coleslaw, or use it as the filling for a delicious sandwich served on a hoagie.

INGREDIENTS | SERVES 4

4 cups ketchup

½ cup apple cider vinegar

1 cup water

½ cup vegan Worcestershire sauce

½ cup light brown sugar, firmly packed

¼ cup molasses

¼ cup prepared mustard

2 tablespoons barbecue seasoning

1 teaspoon freshly ground black pepper

1 tablespoon liquid smoke

1 (14-ounce) package extra-firm tofu, pressed and quartered

1. In a large bowl, combine all the ingredients, except for the tofu. Pour the mixture into a 4-quart slow cooker and add the tofu, making sure that it is fully covered with sauce.

2. Set the slow cooker to high and cook for 1–2 hours, flipping the tofu at the halfway point.

PER SERVING | Calories: 497 | Fat: 3 g | Protein: 12 g | Sodium: 2,080 mg | Fiber: 1.5 g | Carbohydrates: 113 g | Sugar: 97 g

Types of Barbecue Sauce

Barbecue sauce recipes vary greatly by region in the United States, and most fall into one of two categories. They are either vinegar based and have very little sugar, resulting in a thin and somewhat sour taste, or they are tomato based and thick, with a more sweet taste.

Maple-Glazed Tofu

Simple and sweet, like this recipe, is sometimes all you need for a delicious dish!

INGREDIENTS | SERVES 4

4 cloves garlic, minced

1 tablespoon minced ginger

½ cup maple syrup

¼ cup soy sauce

½ cup water

2 tablespoons brown sugar

1 lemon, juiced

¼ teaspoon black pepper

1 (14-ounce) package extra-firm tofu, pressed and quartered

1. In a large bowl, combine all the ingredients, except for the tofu. Pour the mixture into a 4-quart slow cooker and add the tofu.

2. Set the slow cooker to high and cook for 1–2 hours, flipping the tofu at the halfway point.

PER SERVING | Calories: 207 | Fat: 2 g | Protein: 9 g | Sodium: 867 mg | Fiber: 1 g | Carbohydrates: 40 g | Sugar: 32 g

Cracked-Pepper Tofu

Before serving, you can top these tofu fillets with thin slices of fresh lemon, which will perfectly complement the pepper and herbs.

INGREDIENTS | SERVES 4

6 cloves garlic

¼ cup chopped parsley

¼ cup chopped rosemary

¼ cup rice vinegar

½ cup olive oil

¼ cup water

1 teaspoon black pepper

1 (14-ounce) package extra-firm tofu, pressed and quartered

1. In a large bowl, combine all the ingredients, except for the tofu. Pour the mixture into a 4-quart slow cooker and add the tofu.

2. Set the slow cooker to high and cook for 1–2 hours, flipping the tofu at the halfway point.

PER SERVING | Calories: 301 | Fat: 27 g | Protein: 8 g | Sodium: 67 mg | Fiber: 2 g | Carbohydrates: 6 g | Sugar: 1 g

Peanut and Sesame Sauce Tofu

If you are having a hard time combining the ingredients, use a hand mixer or toss them into a blender for about 15 seconds.

INGREDIENTS | SERVES 6

4 cloves garlic, minced

1 tablespoon minced ginger

1 cup creamy peanut butter

1 cup coconut milk

¼ cup unsweetened soymilk

2 tablespoons soy sauce

1 lime, juiced

1 (14-ounce) package extra-firm tofu, pressed and cut into 1-inch cubes

1. In a large bowl, combine all the ingredients, except for the tofu. Pour the mixture into a 4-quart slow cooker and add the tofu.

2. Set the slow cooker to high and cook for 1–2 hours, flipping the tofu at the halfway point.

PER SERVING | Calories: 378 | Fat: 31 g | Protein: 17 g | Sodium: 447 mg | Fiber: 3 g | Carbohydrates: 13 g | Sugar: 5 g

Serving Suggestions

There are endless options for serving Asian-style tofu. Try this tofu as the filling for lettuce wraps, over rice noodles, as the protein on a tasty kebab, or you can play it safe and serve over a bed of steamed rice.

Indian Spinach and Tofu

Traditional Indian dishes often call for cooking the spices over dry heat before using them in a recipe. If you have time, add this step to the recipe.

INGREDIENTS | SERVES 4

2 tablespoons olive oil

4 cloves garlic, minced

1 teaspoon minced ginger

1 cup frozen spinach, thawed and drained

1 tablespoon cumin

1 tablespoon coriander

1 teaspoon turmeric

½ teaspoon red pepper flakes

¼ teaspoon mustard seed

1 (15-ounce) can coconut milk

¼ cup soy sauce

1 (14-ounce) package extra-firm tofu, pressed and quartered

1. Add the olive oil to a 4-quart slow cooker and sauté the garlic and ginger on medium-high heat for 1 minute. Mix in the spinach, cumin, coriander, turmeric, red pepper flakes, mustard seed, coconut milk, and soy sauce.

2. Add the tofu, set the slow cooker to high, and cook for 1–2 hours, flipping the tofu at the halfway point.

PER SERVING | Calories: 358 | Fat: 31 g | Protein: 13 g | Sodium: 906 mg | Fiber: 2.5 g | Carbohydrates: 10 g | Sugar: 1.5 g

CHAPTER 12

Seitan

Spicy Seitan Tacos

Hard or soft taco shells work well with this tasty recipe.

INGREDIENTS | SERVES 8

2 tablespoons olive oil

1 (16-ounce) package seitan, chopped into small pieces

2 cloves garlic, minced

½ cup soy sauce

1 tablespoon chili powder

¼ teaspoon chipotle powder

¼ teaspoon garlic powder

¼ teaspoon crushed red pepper flakes

¼ teaspoon onion powder

2 teaspoons cumin

½ teaspoon paprika

1 teaspoon black pepper

8 taco shells

1 cup shredded lettuce

1 tomato, diced

1. Add all the ingredients, except for shells, lettuce, and tomatoes, to a 4-quart slow cooker. Cover and cook on low heat for 4 hours.

2. Serve the seitan in the shells and top with lettuce and tomato.

PER SERVING | Calories: 193 | Fat: 12 g | Protein: 9.5 g | Sodium: 864 mg | Fiber: 2 g | Carbohydrates: 14 g | Sugar: 1 g

Fresh Tortillas

For an extra special treat, try fresh tortillas. You may have to do a little hunting around, but they can often be found at international farmers' markets and Latino stores.

Jerk Seitan

Many jerk recipes call for rubbing the spice mixture into the protein before cooking, but in a slow cooker that step isn't necessary.

INGREDIENTS | SERVES 4

1 pound shredded seitan

½ cup Vegetable Broth (see Chapter 3)

½ teaspoon allspice

¼ teaspoon cinnamon

½ teaspoon dried thyme

¼ teaspoon ground nutmeg

1 teaspoon salt

¼ cup diced red onion

2 cloves garlic, minced

2 tablespoons seeded and minced, fresh jalapeño

1. Prepare a 4-quart slow cooker with nonstick cooking spray, then add the shredded seitan.

2. In a medium bowl, combine all remaining ingredients. Pour over the seitan.

3. Cover and cook on low for 6 hours.

PER SERVING | Calories: 174 | Fat: 11 g | Protein: 14.5 g | Sodium: 556 mg | Fiber: 1 g | Carbohydrates: 7 g | Sugar: 0.5 g

Seitan Pot Pie

*Gardein Chick'n Strips are a good alternative to seitan in this recipe
and can be found in many major grocery stores.*

INGREDIENTS | SERVES 8

1 (16-ounce) package seitan, cut into bite-sized pieces

4 red potatoes, quartered

2 carrots, peeled and chopped

½ cup chopped celery

½ cup sliced onions

2 (15-ounce) cans vegan cream of mushroom soup

2 teaspoons soy sauce

¼ teaspoon black pepper

Add all the ingredients to a 4-quart slow cooker. Cover and cook on low heat for 6 hours.

PER SERVING | Calories: 248 | Fat: 9 g | Protein: 11 g | Sodium: 448 mg | Fiber: 3 g | Carbohydrates: 29 g | Sugar: 4 g

Homemade Vegan Cream of Mushroom

To make vegan cream of mushroom soup, add 2 tablespoons of a light roux made with unsweetened soymilk and Earth Balance Original Buttery Spread to 2 cups unsweetened soymilk, and then add sautéed mushrooms and onions.

Stroganoff

The beef commonly used in stroganoff can be replaced with mushrooms, tempeh, or seitan to create a vegan dish.

INGREDIENTS | SERVES 8

1 tablespoon extra-virgin olive oil

1 yellow onion, diced

2 cloves garlic, minced

1 pound seitan, chopped

1 teaspoon salt

4 cups Vegetable Broth (see Chapter 3)

½ cup vegan sour cream

1 tablespoon ground mustard

¼ cup chopped parsley

1 pound cooked linguine or fettuccine pasta

1. Heat the olive oil in a sauté pan over medium heat. Add the onion and garlic, and cook for 2 minutes.

2. Place the sautéed onion and garlic, seitan, salt, and Vegetable Broth in a 4-quart slow cooker. Cover and cook on low for 7 hours.

3. In a small bowl, combine the sour cream, mustard, and parsley. Add to the slow cooker, stirring well.

4. Cover and cook on low for an additional 15 minutes. Serve over cooked pasta.

PER SERVING | Calories: 197 g | Fat: 7 g | Protein: 8 g | Sodium: 467 mg | Fiber: 1.5 g | Carbohydrates: 21 g | Sugar: 2 g

Spiced Apple Cider Seitan

This recipe makes candied sweet potatoes while it cooks the seitan in the sweetened cider sauce.

INGREDIENTS | SERVES 8

3 pounds seitan, cubed

¼ teaspoon salt

¼ teaspoon pepper

2 apples, peeled, cored, and sliced

4 large sweet potatoes, peeled and cut in half

½ cup apple cider or apple juice

½ teaspoon ground cinnamon

¼ teaspoon ground cloves

¼ teaspoon ground allspice

2 tablespoons brown sugar

1. Treat the crock of a 4-quart slow cooker with nonstick spray.

2. Add seitan and season it with salt and pepper.

3. Arrange apple slices over and around the seitan. Add the sweet potatoes.

4. In a bowl or measuring cup, stir together the cider or juice, cinnamon, cloves, allspice, and brown sugar. Pour over the ingredients in the slow cooker.

5. Cover and cook on low for 8 hours.

PER SERVING | Calories: 369 | Fat: 17 g | Protein: 23 g | Sodium: 60 mg | Fiber: 4.5 g | Carbohydrates: 37 g | Sugar: 13 g

Apples-and-Onions Seitan

Try Sonya apples in this sweet and savory dish; they are crisp and sweet.

INGREDIENTS | SERVES 4

4 crisp sweet apples, cut into wedges

2 large onions, sliced

1 cup water

4 equal-sized seitan cutlets (about 1 pound total)

½ teaspoon ground cayenne

½ teaspoon ground cinnamon

¼ teaspoon allspice

¼ teaspoon ground fennel

1. Place half of the apple wedges and half of the sliced onions in the bottom of a 4-quart slow cooker, then add water. Top with a single layer of seitan.

2. Sprinkle with spices, and top with the remaining apples and onions.

3. Cover and cook on low for 8 hours.

PER SERVING | Calories: 178 | Fat: 3.5 g | Protein: 9 g | Sodium: 43 mg | Fiber: 3.5 g | Carbohydrates: 30 g | Sugar: 20 g

In Season

Apples are in peak season only once a year, so grab your basket and head to the orchard during the fall. However, you can find good apples during other seasons, too. Just check your local supermarket.

Red Wine "Pot Roast"

A little bit of wine goes a long way in flavoring this simple one-crock meal.

INGREDIENTS | SERVES 6

⅓ cup red wine
½ cup water
4 red skin potatoes, quartered
3 carrots, cut into thirds
2 bulbs fennel, quartered
2 rutabagas, quartered
1 onion, sliced
4 cloves garlic, sliced
1½ pounds seitan, cubed
½ teaspoon salt
½ teaspoon freshly ground black pepper

1. Pour the wine and water into a 4-quart slow cooker. Add the potatoes, carrots, fennel, rutabagas, onion, and garlic. Stir.

2. Add the seitan. Sprinkle with salt and pepper. Cover and cook on low for 8 hours.

PER SERVING | Calories: 378 | Fat: 12 g | Protein: 20 g | Sodium: 300 mg | Fiber: 11 g | Carbohydrates: 49 g | Sugar: 11 g

Seitan Fricassee

*A fricassee is a versatile dish that is easily adapted for personal taste.
Fennel, mushrooms, or parsnips can be used with great success.*

INGREDIENTS | SERVES 6

2 cups sliced red cabbage
2 carrots, cut into coin-sized pieces
2 stalks celery, diced
1 onion, sliced
1 pound seitan, cut into large cubes
¾ cup faux chicken stock
2 teaspoons paprika
2 teaspoons dried thyme
2 teaspoons dried parsley

1. Place the cabbage, carrots, celery, and onion on the bottom of a 4-quart slow cooker. Place the seitan on top of the vegetables.

2. Pour the stock over the seitan, and sprinkle it evenly with the spices. Pat the spices onto the seitan.

3. Cook on low 6 hours or until the seitan is cooked through.

PER SERVING | Calories: 107 | Fat: 2.5 g | Protein: 7 g | Sodium: 191 mg | Fiber: 2 g | Carbohydrates: 9.5 g | Sugar: 4 g

Moroccan "Chicken"

This dish was inspired by traditional North African tagines and adapted for the slow cooker.

INGREDIENTS | SERVES 8

½ teaspoon coriander

½ teaspoon cinnamon

¼ teaspoon salt

1 teaspoon cumin

2 pounds seitan, cubed

½ cup water

4 cloves garlic, minced

1 onion, thinly sliced

1 knob ginger, minced

1 (15-ounce) can chickpeas, drained and rinsed

4 ounces dried apricots, halved

1. Place all of the spices, seitan, water, garlic, onion, and ginger into a 4-quart slow cooker. Cook on low for 5 hours.

2. Stir in the chickpeas and apricots and cook on high for 40 minutes.

PER SERVING | Calories: 323 | Fat: 6 g | Protein: 19 g | Sodium: 129 mg | Fiber: 11 g | Carbohydrates: 45 g | Sugar: 15 g

Moroccan Cuisine

Moroccan cuisine uses many different spices. Some of the most common are cumin, cinnamon, turmeric, saffron, and paprika. Traditional Moroccan food is served in a communal bowl at a low, round table. Diners take food from the bowl using pieces of bread or their hands.

Vegan Ropa Vieja

Serve this Cuban dish with yellow rice and black beans.
It also makes a great filling for corn or flour tortillas.

INGREDIENTS | SERVES 8

2 pounds seitan, cubed

1 cubanelle pepper, diced

1 large onion, diced

2 carrots, diced

2 (15-ounce) cans canned crushed tomatoes

2 cloves garlic

1 teaspoon dried oregano

½ teaspoon cumin

½ cup sliced green olives stuffed with pimento

1. Add all of the ingredients to a 4-quart slow cooker. Cook on low for 7 hours.

2. Shred the seitan with a fork, knife, or grater, then mash it with a potato masher until very well mixed.

PER SERVING | Calories: 210 | Fat: 12 g | Protein: 15.5 g | Sodium: 229 mg | Fiber: 3 g | Carbohydrates: 14 g | Sugar: 4 g

All about Cumin

Cumin is a spice made from the seed of a plant of the same name. It is dried and ground before use and gives a strong earthy, and somewhat nutty, flavor to dishes.

Cashew Seitan

Hoisin is a soy-based, sweet-and-spicy sauce that is often used as a glaze for meats in Chinese dishes.

INGREDIENTS | SERVES 6

¼ cup rice wine

½ cup hoisin sauce

¼ cup soy sauce

½ cup water

1 tablespoon sugar

2 tablespoons olive oil

1 red bell pepper, chopped

1 green bell pepper, chopped

4 cloves garlic, minced

1 (16-ounce) package seitan, cut into bite-sized pieces

½ cup cashew pieces

1. Combine the rice wine, hoisin, soy sauce, water, and sugar in a 4-quart slow cooker. Stir well, and then add all remaining ingredients, except for the cashews.

2. Cover and cook on low for 6 hours. Garnish with cashew pieces before serving.

PER SERVING | Calories: 274 | Fat: 15 g | Protein: 12 g | Sodium: 848 mg | Fiber: 2 g | Carbohydrates: 20 g | Sugar: 9 g

Middle Eastern Lemon Seitan

In Middle Eastern cuisine, chickpeas are most commonly used in hummus, but they are also delicious when left whole and slow cooked in a rich sauce.

INGREDIENTS | SERVES 6

1 lemon, juiced
1 (15-ounce) can diced tomatoes
1 (15-ounce) can chickpeas, drained
½ cup water
1 teaspoon cumin
1 teaspoon coriander
4 garlic cloves, minced
½ teaspoon cinnamon
½ teaspoon salt
1 (16-ounce) package seitan, cut into bite-sized pieces

Add all of the ingredients to a 4-quart slow cooker. Cover and cook on low heat for 6 hours.

PER SERVING | Calories: 241 | Fat: 9 g | Protein: 16 g | Sodium: 304 mg | Fiber: 6.5 g | Carbohydrates: 26 g | Sugar: 5 g

Being Vegan in the Middle East

The concept of veganism is still very far from being widely accepted in the Middle East, but that doesn't mean there isn't plenty for vegans to eat when sampling the cuisine. Several dishes are naturally vegan, such as baba ganoush and tabouli.

Braised Seitan with Mushrooms

The best gravies are usually made with the drippings, or leftover liquid from a cooked dish.
They are packed with flavor and guaranteed to complement the meal.

INGREDIENTS | SERVES 6

1 cup sliced mushrooms

4 cups water

2 tablespoons Better Than Bouillon No Beef Base

½ cup red wine

1 teaspoon dried tarragon or thyme

1 teaspoon salt

¼ teaspoon black pepper

1 (16-ounce) package seitan, cut into bite-sized pieces

2 tablespoons cornstarch, dissolved in ⅛ cup 2 tablespoons water

1. Add all of the ingredients except for the cornstarch to a 4-quart slow cooker. Cover and cook on low heat for 6 hours.

2. Use a slotted spoon to remove the seitan from the slow cooker and set aside. Whisk in the cornstarch until it creates a gravy consistency, and then serve the mushroom gravy over the braised seitan.

PER SERVING | Calories: 138 | Fat: 7 g | Protein: 10 g | Sodium: 350 mg | Fiber: 1 g | Carbohydrates: 6.5 g | Sugar: 0.3 g

Seitan Cacciatore

Cacciatore style typically means a piece of meat that is seared and then slow cooked with tomatoes, herbs, and wine, but you can veganize it by opting for tempeh, tofu, or seitan as the protein.

INGREDIENTS | SERVES 6

2 tablespoons olive oil

1 (16-ounce) package seitan, cut into bite-sized pieces

1 onion, chopped

1 red bell pepper, chopped

1 green bell pepper, chopped

4 cloves garlic, minced

1 (28-ounce) can diced tomatoes

1 cup Vegetable Broth (see Chapter 3)

2 tablespoons soy sauce

½ cup white wine

¼ teaspoon black pepper

2 tablespoons cornstarch, dissolved in 2 tablespoons water

¼ cup chopped basil

1. Add the olive oil to a large sauté pan on medium heat and sauté the seitan for 3–5 minutes. Add the onion, bell peppers, and garlic, and sauté for an additional 3 minutes, then transfer to a 4-quart slow cooker.

2. Add the tomatoes, Vegetable Broth, soy sauce, white wine, and black pepper. Cover and cook on low heat for 6 hours.

3. With a slotted spoon, remove the seitan from the slow cooker and set aside. Whisk in the cornstarch until it creates a sauce consistency. Garnish with the chopped basil before serving.

PER SERVING | Calories: 186 | Fat: 8 g | Protein: 11 g | Sodium: 307 mg | Fiber: 3 g | Carbohydrates: 17 g | Sugar: 6 g

Skip the Alcohol

If you'd like to leave the alcohol out of this dish, it's easy to substitute it with another liquid. Simply replace it with an additional ½ cup of Vegetable Broth.

Garlic Seitan

Garlic has many health benefits and is said to protect against certain types of cancer and heart disease.

INGREDIENTS | SERVES 6

½ cup olive oil

4 garlic cloves, crushed

1 (16-ounce) package seitan, cut into 4 fillets

1 cup panko bread crumbs

1 teaspoon salt

¼ teaspoon black pepper

1. Add the olive oil, garlic, and seitan to a medium bowl and allow the seitan to marinate for 5 minutes.

2. In a separate bowl, mix the bread crumbs, salt, and pepper. Dip the seitan into the bread crumbs and place in a 4-quart slow cooker.

3. Pour the oil and garlic marinade into the slow cooker. Cover and cook on high for 2 hours. Flip the seitan halfway through cooking.

PER SERVING | Calories: 342 | Fat: 26 g | Protein: 12 g | Sodium: 426 mg | Fiber: 1.5 g | Carbohydrates: 16 g | Sugar: 1 g

Italian Herb Seitan

Serve this simple Italian dish over a bed of angel hair pasta and use the remaining liquid as a sauce to dress your pasta.

INGREDIENTS | SERVES 6

1 (16-ounce) package seitan, cut into bite-sized pieces

6 cloves garlic, minced

¼ cup rice wine vinegar

½ cup Vegetable Broth (see Chapter 3)

½ cup chopped rosemary

½ cup chopped parsley

1 teaspoon salt

¼ teaspoon black pepper

Add all of the ingredients to a 4-quart slow cooker. Cover and cook on low heat for 6 hours.

PER SERVING | Calories: 130 | Fat: 8 g | Protein: 10 g | Sodium: 345 mg | Fiber: 2.5 g | Carbohydrates: 7.5 g | Sugar: 0 g

The Power of Seitan

Seitan, otherwise known as wheat gluten, is a powerful source of protein and a great alternative to meat. One serving has a whopping 18 grams of protein, and the benefits don't stop there—it's also a great source of iron.

Seitan Provençal

This dish is a vegan take on the popular Chicken Provençal, and like many Provençal dishes, it is full of Mediterranean ingredients, such as olives, garlic, and herbs.

INGREDIENTS | SERVES 6

1 (16-ounce) package seitan, cut into bite-sized pieces

1 (28-ounce) can diced tomatoes

½ cup white wine

1 cup Vegetable Broth (see Chapter 3)

4 cloves garlic, minced

¼ cup pitted and chopped kalamata olives

1 teaspoon salt

¼ teaspoon black pepper

¼ cup chopped, fresh basil

1. Add all ingredients, except for the basil, to a 4-quart slow cooker. Cover and cook on low heat for 6 hours.

2. Sprinkle with basil just before serving.

PER SERVING | Calories: 158 | Fat: 7.5 g | Protein: 10 g | Sodium: 523 mg | Fiber: 2 g | Carbohydrates: 11 g | Sugar: 3.5 g

Adobo Seitan

*Serve this dish over steamed white rice, which will help balance out
the strong acidic flavor from the vinegar.*

INGREDIENTS | SERVES 6

½ cup soy sauce

1 cup white vinegar

1 cup water

4 cloves garlic, minced

1 teaspoon minced ginger

4 bay leaves

1 teaspoon paprika

10 black peppercorns

1 (16-ounce) package seitan, cut into bite-sized pieces

Add all ingredients to a 4-quart slow cooker. Cover and cook on high for 2 hours.

PER SERVING | Calories: 132 | Fat: 7.5 g | Protein: 11 g | Sodium: 1,152 mg | Fiber: 1 g | Carbohydrates: 6 g | Sugar: 0.5 g

Spanish Versus Filipino Adobo

There are Spanish and Filipino dishes that share the name adobo, but the two are slightly different. Both share the ingredients of vinegar and garlic, but the Spanish version mostly refers to a marinade that is used before cooking, and the Filipino version is a cooking method.

Mandarin Seitan

Surprisingly, this vegan take on mandarin chicken doesn't call for mandarin oranges at all!

INGREDIENTS | SERVES 6

4 cloves garlic, minced

1 teaspoon minced ginger

1 (16-ounce) package seitan, cut into bite-sized pieces

½ cup soy sauce

⅓ cup sugar

1 lemon, juiced

1 cup water

2 tablespoons cornstarch, dissolved in 2 tablespoons water

1. Add all of the ingredients, except for the cornstarch, to a 4-quart slow cooker. Cover and cook on high for 2 hours.

2. Remove the seitan with a slotted spoon. Whisk in the cornstarch until the liquid has the consistency of a sauce. Serve over rice.

PER SERVING | Calories: 180 | Fat: 7 g | Protein: 11 g | Sodium: 1,101 mg | Fiber: 1 g | Carbohydrates: 20 g | Sugar: 11 g

Seitan Scaloppini

Scaloppini traditionally calls for coating the protein in bread crumbs before cooking,
but in this slow cooker version, you sprinkle them on top after cooking.

INGREDIENTS | SERVES 6

1 (16-ounce) package seitan, cut into 6 thin fillets

1 lemon, juiced

1 cup water

1 tablespoon Better Than Bouillon No Chicken Base

¼ cup white wine

¼ cup capers

¼ teaspoon black pepper

1 cup toasted panko bread crumbs

¼ cup chopped parsley

1. Add the seitan, lemon juice, water, "chicken" base, white wine, capers, and black pepper to a 4-quart slow cooker. Cover and cook on low heat for 4–6 hours.

2. Remove the seitan from the slow cooker and garnish with toasted bread crumbs and chopped parsley before serving.

PER SERVING | Calories: 183 | Fat: 8 g | Protein: 12 g | Sodium: 306 mg | Fiber: 2 g | Carbohydrates: 17 g | Sugar: 1.5 g

Seitan Cuban Sandwich

*Cuban sandwiches are often pressed after assembly. No need for
a panini press or grill pan though, just use your hand!*

INGREDIENTS | SERVES 4

1 (16-ounce) package seitan, thinly sliced

6 oranges, juiced

6 limes, juiced

½ teaspoon cumin

1 teaspoon dried oregano

½ teaspoon lemon pepper

2 tablespoons soy sauce

¼ cup olive oil

1 loaf Cuban bread, sliced in half

4 slices vegan pepper jack cheese

12 dill pickle slices

4 teaspoons mustard

1. Add all of the ingredients, except for the bread, cheese, pickles, and mustard, to a 4-quart slow cooker. Cover and cook the seitan on high heat for 1–2 hours.

2. Remove the slices of seitan with tongs and assemble the sandwiches on the bread by layering the seitan, cheese, pickles, and mustard.

PER SERVING | Calories: 645 | Fat: 35 g | Protein: 29 g | Sodium: 701 mg | Fiber: 9 g | Carbohydrates: 63 g | Sugar: 21 g

CHAPTER 13

Tempeh

Ginger-Soy Tempeh Cubes

Tempeh is made from fermented soybeans and is used as a meat replacement in many vegan dishes.

INGREDIENTS | SERVES 4

3 cloves garlic, minced

1 tablespoon minced, fresh ginger

½ cup soy sauce

1 cup water

2 limes, juiced

¼ cup olive oil

2 tablespoons sugar

1 (13-ounce) package tempeh, cut into bite-sized squares

3 green onions, sliced

1. In a small bowl, combine garlic, ginger, soy sauce, water, lime juice, olive oil, and sugar.

2. Add the garlic mixture and tempeh to a 4-quart slow cooker. Cover and cook on medium heat for 4 hours. Garnish with the green onions.

PER SERVING | Calories: 353 | Fat: 23 g | Protein: 19 g | Sodium: 1,509 mg | Fiber: 1.5 g | Carbohydrates: 22 g | Sugar: 7 g

Tempeh Reuben Sandwiches

Some grocery-store-brand Thousand Island dressings are "accidentally vegan,"
just be sure to read the label.

INGREDIENTS | SERVES 6

1 (13-ounce) package tempeh, cut into strips

1 cup water

¼ cup apple cider vinegar

2 tablespoons paprika

1 tablespoon dried oregano

¼ cup Dijon mustard

¼ teaspoon liquid smoke

2 teaspoons allspice

3 cloves garlic, minced

1 teaspoon salt

¼ teaspoon black pepper

12 slices rye bread

1 cup sauerkraut

6 slices vegan Cheddar cheese

½ cup Thousand Island dressing

1. Add the tempeh, water, apple cider vinegar, paprika, oregano, Dijon mustard, liquid smoke, allspice, garlic, salt, and pepper to a 4-quart slow cooker. Cover and cook on medium heat for 4 hours.

2. Serve on the rye bread with sauerkraut, cheese, and Thousand Island dressing.

PER SERVING | Calories: 500 | Fat: 26 g | Protein: 25 g | Sodium: 1,327 mg | Fiber: 5 g | Carbohydrates: 43 g | Sugar: 6.5 g

Curried Tempeh in Coconut Cream

Try serving this curried tempeh over rice or in cool, crisp lettuce leaves.

INGREDIENTS | SERVES 4

2 cloves garlic, minced

1 teaspoon minced, fresh ginger

¼ cup soy sauce

1 tablespoon vegetable oil

1 tablespoon sriracha sauce

1 (13-ounce) can coconut milk

1 cup water

1 (13-ounce) package tempeh, cut into bite-sized squares

¼ cup chopped fresh basil

1. Add all ingredients, except for the basil, to a 4-quart slow cooker. Cover and cook on low heat for 6 hours.

2. About 10 minutes before the tempeh is done cooking, stir in the basil. Cook for the remaining time and serve.

PER SERVING | Calories: 397 | Fat: 32 g | Protein: 20 g | Sodium: 913 mg | Fiber: 0.5 g | Carbohydrates: 13 g | Sugar: 0.5 g

Tempeh Braised in Sauerkraut

Sauerkraut is fermented cabbage that is often sold canned or in jars in grocery stores nationwide.

INGREDIENTS | SERVES 6

3 cups sauerkraut

½ tablespoon caraway seeds

1 tablespoon yellow mustard seeds

1 small onion, thinly sliced

2 tablespoons apple cider vinegar

1 pound tempeh, cut into 1½-inch cubes

1. Place the sauerkraut, caraway seeds, mustard seeds, onions, and vinegar into a 4- or 6-quart slow cooker. Stir to distribute all ingredients evenly.

2. Add the tempeh and toss.

3. Cover and cook for 3–4 hours on low.

PER SERVING | Calories: 179 | Fat: 8.5 g | Protein: 15 g | Sodium: 416 mg | Fiber: 2.5 g | Carbohydrates: 12 g | Sugar: 2 g

Spicy Tempeh Fajitas

Add a dollop of soy sour cream and salsa to finish off each of your fajitas.

INGREDIENTS | SERVES 4

1 (13-ounce) package tempeh, cut into bite-sized pieces

2 cloves garlic, minced

1 teaspoon minced fresh ginger

¼ cup soy sauce

1 cup water

1 tablespoon olive oil

½ teaspoon chili powder

¼ teaspoon chipotle powder

¼ teaspoon black pepper

½ onion, sliced

½ green bell pepper, sliced

1 jalapeño, minced

½ cup sliced mushrooms

8–12 corn tortillas

1 tomato, diced

¼ cup chopped cilantro

1 lime, cut into wedges

1. Add the tempeh, garlic, ginger, soy sauce, water, olive oil, chili powder, chipotle powder, black pepper, onion, green bell pepper, jalapeño, and mushrooms to a 4-quart slow cooker. Cover and cook on low heat for 6 hours.

2. Serve the fajitas on the tortillas and garnish with tomato, cilantro, and lime.

PER SERVING | Calories: 357 | Fat: 15 g | Protein: 22 g | Sodium: 840 mg | Fiber: 5 g | Carbohydrates: 39 g | Sugar: 3 g

Buffalo Tempeh

This recipe makes appetizer-size servings, not full entrée-size servings.

INGREDIENTS | SERVES 8

1 (13-ounce) package tempeh, cut into strips

1 cup melted Earth Balance Original Buttery Spread

1 cup Tabasco sauce

3 stalks celery, cut into strips

1 cup vegan ranch dressing

1. Add the tempeh, Earth Balance, and Tabasco sauce to a 4-quart slow cooker. Cover and cook on low heat for 6 hours.

2. Serve on a platter with the celery sticks and dressing.

PER SERVING | Calories: 439 | Fat: 43 g | Protein: 10 g | Sodium: 476 mg | Fiber: 0.5 g | Carbohydrates: 6.5 g | Sugar: 1.5 g

Vegan Ranch

Vegan ranch dressing is sold in some grocery stores and can be ordered online. Try Organicville's Non Dairy Ranch Organic Dressing as a delicious alternative to traditional ranch.

Tempeh Sausage Crumbles

*For a healthier alternative to store-bought faux sausage,
you can make your own using crumbled tempeh.*

INGREDIENTS | SERVES 4

1 (13-ounce) package tempeh, crumbled

2 tablespoons olive oil

¼ cup water

4 cloves garlic, minced

1 tablespoon dried sage

¼ teaspoon dried marjoram

2 tablespoons brown sugar

¼ teaspoon crushed red pepper

1 teaspoon salt

¼ teaspoon black pepper

Add all ingredients to a 4-quart slow cooker. Cover and cook on high heat for 2 hours.

PER SERVING | Calories: 267 | Fat: 16 g | Protein: 17 g | Sodium: 500 mg | Fiber: 0.3 g | Carbohydrates: 16 g | Sugar: 6 g

"Short Rib" Tempeh

No pigs are necessary for this mouthwatering "rib" recipe!

INGREDIENTS | SERVES 4

1 (13-ounce) package tempeh, cut into strips

1 (28-ounce) can tomato sauce

½ cup water

2 tablespoons vegan Worcestershire sauce

2 tablespoons brown sugar

2 tablespoons dried parsley

1 teaspoon Tabasco sauce

¼ teaspoon black pepper

1 lemon, juiced

1 tablespoon soy sauce

Add all ingredients to a 4-quart slow cooker. Cover and cook on low heat for 6 hours.

PER SERVING | Calories: 264 | Fat: 10 g | Protein: 20 g | Sodium: 1,157 mg | Fiber: 3.5 g | Carbohydrates: 29 g | Sugar: 16 g

Tempeh Tamale Pie

In a slight variation from the baked classic, this version of tamale pie features plump, moist cornmeal dumplings.

INGREDIENTS | SERVES 4

2 tablespoons olive oil

1 large onion, minced

1 pound tempeh, crumbled

1 jalapeño, minced

2 cloves garlic, minced

1 (15-ounce) can diced tomatoes

1 (10-ounce) can diced tomatoes with green chilies

1 (15-ounce) can dark red kidney beans, drained and rinsed

4 chipotle peppers in adobo, minced

½ teaspoon hot Mexican chili powder

⅔ cup unsweetened soymilk

2 tablespoons canola oil

2 teaspoons baking powder

½ cup cornmeal

½ teaspoon salt

1. In a large sauté pan over medium heat, add the olive oil. Sauté the onion, tempeh, jalapeño, and garlic for 5 minutes.

2. Pour the tempeh mixture into a 4-quart slow cooker. Add the tomatoes, tomatoes with green chilies, beans, chipotle peppers, and chili powder. Cover and cook on low for 8 hours.

3. In a medium bowl, mix the soymilk, oil, baking powder, cornmeal, and salt. Drop ¼-cup mounds in a single layer on top of the tempeh.

4. Cover and cook on high for 20 minutes without lifting the lid. The dumplings will look fluffy and light when fully cooked.

PER SERVING | Calories: 635 | Fat: 27 g | Protein: 36 g | Sodium: 689 mg | Fiber: 16 g | Carbohydrates: 67 g | Sugar: 9 g

Canned Versus Fresh Tomatoes

While fresh tomatoes are delicious, canned tomatoes are a better choice in some recipes because they have already been cooked, and their skins and seeds have been removed. There is also reason to believe that canned tomatoes are better sources of cancer-preventing lycopene simply because they are cooked, and that one can of crushed tomatoes or sauce is the equivalent of dozens of fresh tomatoes.

Lemon-Pepper Tempeh

When fresh herbs are in season, add chopped curly
or flat-leaf parsley to this dish before serving.

INGREDIENTS | SERVES 4

1 (13-ounce) package tempeh, cut into bite-sized squares

6 cloves garlic, minced

1 teaspoon minced fresh ginger

¾ cup water

¼ cup soy sauce

½ cup extra-virgin olive oil

¼ cup fresh lemon juice

1 teaspoon black pepper

Add all ingredients to a 4-quart slow cooker. Cover and cook on low heat for 6 hours.

PER SERVING | Calories: 433 | Fat: 36 g | Protein: 18 g | Sodium: 812 mg | Fiber: 0 g | Carbohydrates: 12 g | Sugar: 0.5 g

Serving Suggestions

Make this tempeh dish the star of the show and serve as a main course with a vegetable and grain on the side. Or, place the strips on a hoagie roll topped with vegan mayonnaise and lettuce to make a tasty sub sandwich.

Sriracha and Soy Tempeh

Sriracha is sometimes affectionately referred to as "rooster sauce" because of the drawing on the bottle of Huy Fong's sriracha sauce, but don't let the cute name fool you. This sauce packs a spicy punch.

INGREDIENTS | SERVES 4

1 (13-ounce) package tempeh, cut into bite-sized squares

4 cloves garlic, minced

1 teaspoon minced ginger

1 tablespoon olive oil

½ cup soy sauce

¼ cup water

2 tablespoons brown sugar

1 teaspoon sriracha sauce

Add all ingredients to a 4-quart slow cooker. Cover and cook on high heat for 2 hours.

PER SERVING | Calories: 254 | Fat: 13 g | Protein: 19 g | Sodium: 1,698 mg | Fiber: 0.3 g | Carbohydrates: 19 g | Sugar: 7 g

Orange-Pomegranate Tempeh Bites

Pomegranate juice is a good source of vitamin C, and though the official verdict is still under debate, it may be a good source of antioxidants, too.

INGREDIENTS | SERVES 4

1 (13-ounce) package tempeh, cut into bite-sized squares

1 tablespoon olive oil

¼ cup soy sauce

¼ teriyaki glaze

2 tablespoons brown sugar

3 oranges, juiced

¼ cup pomegranate juice

Add all ingredients to a 4-quart slow cooker. Cover and cook on high heat for 2 hours.

PER SERVING | Calories: 293 | Fat: 13 g | Protein: 18 g | Sodium: 809 mg | Fiber: 2.5 g | Carbohydrates: 29 g | Sugar: 17 g

Tempeh Sliders

Sliders are mini sandwiches, perfect as an appetizer or a snack.

INGREDIENTS | SERVES 4

1 (13-ounce) package tempeh, cut into 8 squares

2 cloves garlic, minced

1 teaspoon minced, fresh ginger

¼ cup soy sauce

1 cup water

¼ teaspoon black pepper

½ teaspoon garlic powder

½ teaspoon onion powder

¼ teaspoon cumin

⅛ teaspoon cayenne pepper

2 teaspoons olive oil

½ onion, sliced

8 slices vegan Cheddar cheese

8 mini sandwich buns

1. Add the tempeh, garlic, ginger, soy sauce, water, black pepper, garlic powder, onion powder, cumin, and cayenne pepper to a 4-quart slow cooker. Cover and cook on low heat for 6 hours.

2. About 5 minutes before the sliders are done cooking, add the olive oil to a pan and sauté the onions over medium-high heat until they are soft, about 5 minutes.

3. Melt a slice of cheese on each piece of tempeh and top with the onions. Serve on mini sandwich buns.

PER SERVING | Calories: 489 | Fat: 23 g | Protein: 37 g | Sodium: 1,325 mg | Fiber: 4.5 g | Carbohydrates: 41 g | Sugar: 6 g

Finding Vegan Bread

Some bread recipes call for eggs, dairy, and honey, but there are also many that do not, and finding vegan sandwich buns shouldn't be a challenge. Some grocery stores such as Kroger even label Kroger-brand bread as vegan if it is.

Pesto-Marinated Tempeh

What goes better with pesto than an al dente pasta!

INGREDIENTS | SERVES 4

¼ cup olive oil

2 cloves garlic

2 cups basil

¼ cup pine nuts, toasted

1 cup water

1 (13-ounce) package tempeh, cut into bite-sized squares

How to Toast Pine Nuts

Toasting pine nuts is quite simple. All you need is a dry sauté pan! Bring the pan to medium heat, add the nuts, and gently stir them so that the nuts toast evenly. Be careful not to burn the nuts; they should be removed from the heat as they begin to turn a light brown color.

1. Place the olive oil, garlic, basil, and toasted pines nuts into a food processor and purée to make the pesto.

2. Pour the pesto, water, and tempeh into a 4-quart slow cooker. Cover and cook on low heat for 6 hours.

PER SERVING | Calories: 390 | Fat: 32 g | Protein: 19 g | Sodium: 21 mg | Fiber: 2 g | Carbohydrates: 12 g | Sugar: 0 g

Tempeh and Greens

*Collard greens are a Southern staple, but if you prefer
a more tender green, opt for kale instead.*

INGREDIENTS | SERVES 6

1 (13-ounce) package tempeh, cut into bite-sized squares

4 cloves garlic

1 onion, chopped

8 cups stemmed and chopped collard greens

1 teaspoon Better Than Bouillon No Chicken Base

4 cups water

2 tablespoons soy sauce

1 teaspoon hot sauce

1 teaspoon salt

¼ teaspoon black pepper

Add all ingredients to a 4-quart slow cooker. Cover and cook on low heat for 6 hours. Use a slotted spoon to serve the tempeh and greens in a bowl.

PER SERVING | Calories: 144 | Fat: 6 g | Protein: 13 g | Sodium: 734 mg | Fiber: 2 g | Carbohydrates: 11 g | Sugar: 1 g

Cajun Tempeh Po' Boys

This recipe makes two very large sandwiches,
so bring your appetite or you can save some for later.

INGREDIENTS | SERVES 2

1 (13-ounce) package tempeh, cut into small bite-sized squares

½ cup olive oil

5 cloves garlic, minced

1 onion, chopped

2 teaspoons oregano

2 teaspoons thyme

2 teaspoons cayenne pepper

2 tablespoons paprika

1 teaspoon salt

¼ teaspoon black pepper

1 loaf French bread, sliced horizontally

2 cups shredded lettuce

2 tomatoes, sliced

1. Add all ingredients, except for the bread, lettuce, and tomato, to a 4-quart slow cooker. Cover and cook on high heat for 2 hours.

2. Assemble the sandwiches on the bread by layering the tempeh, lettuce, and tomatoes.

PER SERVING | Calories: 1163 | Fat: 76 g | Protein: 47 g | Sodium: 1,037 mg | Fiber: 8 g | Carbohydrates: 84 g | Sugar: 9 g

All "Dressed" Up

Traditional New Orleans po' boys are served either plain or dressed. Dressed means it's topped with lettuce, tomatoes, pickles, and mayo, but you can substitute Vegenaise to keep the sandwich vegan.

Tempeh Pot Pie

Some brands of frozen puff pastry are "accidentally vegan."
Just be sure to read the ingredients before purchasing.

INGREDIENTS | SERVES 4

½ cup Earth Balance Original Buttery Spread
1 onion, chopped
2 carrots, peeled and chopped
1 cup chopped mushrooms
½ cup flour
1 cup unsweetened soymilk
1 cup frozen peas
1 (13-ounce) package tempeh, cut into bite-sized squares
½ cup water
2 teaspoons lemon pepper
1 teaspoon salt
¼ teaspoon black pepper
1 sheet frozen puff pastry, cut into 4 squares

1. Add the Earth Balance to a large sauté pan over medium heat. Once melted, add the onion, carrots, and mushrooms, and sauté for 3–5 minutes.

2. Add the flour and whisk to create a roux, then slowly whisk in the soymilk and stir until all lumps have been removed.

3. Transfer the contents of the sauté pan to a 4-quart slow cooker and add all remaining ingredients, except for the puff pastry. Cover and cook on low heat for 6 hours.

4. Meanwhile, cook the puff pastry according to package directions, or until it is golden brown. Serve the pot pie in a bowl and top each bowl with one piece of the puff pastry.

PER SERVING | Calories: 451 | Fat: 25 g | Protein: 24 g | Sodium: 799 mg | Fiber: 4 g | Carbohydrates: 36 g | Sugar: 5.6 g

Tempeh Jambalaya

Unlike the famous New Orleans dish gumbo, jambalaya isn't meant to be brothy.
Instead, you should cook the rice dish until all of the liquid is absorbed.

INGREDIENTS | SERVES 6

1 (13-ounce) package tempeh, cut into bite-sized squares

1 onion, chopped

2 stalks celery, chopped

1 bell pepper, chopped

4 cloves garlic, minced

2 cups uncooked white rice

2 teaspoons Better Than Bouillon No Chicken Base

5 cups water

1 (15-ounce) can tomato sauce

2 bay leaves

2 tablespoons Cajun seasoning

¼ teaspoon dried thyme

2 teaspoons hot sauce

1 teaspoon salt

¼ teaspoon black pepper

Add all ingredients to a 4-quart slow cooker. Cover and cook on low heat for 6 hours or until all of the liquid is absorbed.

PER SERVING | Calories: 389 | Fat: 7 g | Protein: 17 g | Sodium: 825 mg | Fiber: 3.5 g | Carbohydrates: 65 g | Sugar: 4.5 g

Jambalaya Variations

There are two variations of jambalaya made throughout Louisiana—Creole and Cajun. The Creole version is tomato based, while the Cajun version omits tomatoes in favor of more gamey meats, making it more difficult to veganize.

Tempeh Mole

Mole is a type of Mexican sauce that is used on a variety of proteins. Try serving this Tempeh Mole over a bed of rice or with warm flour tortillas.

INGREDIENTS | SERVES 4

2 tablespoons olive oil

1 onion, chopped

4 cloves garlic, minced

2 tablespoons flour

2 teaspoons Better Than Bouillon No Chicken Base

3 cups water

2 tablespoons chili powder

1 teaspoon cumin

1 teaspoon dried oregano

½ teaspoon cinnamon

⅓ cup vegan chocolate chips

½ teaspoon salt

⅛ teaspoon black pepper

1 (13-ounce) package tempeh, cut into bite-sized squares

1. Place the olive oil in a sauté pan over medium heat. Add the onion and garlic, and sauté for 2–3 minutes. When done, add the flour and whisk to create a roux.

2. Transfer the roux mixture and all remaining ingredients to a 4-quart slow cooker. Cover and cook on high for 2 hours.

PER SERVING | Calories: 347 | Fat: 21 g | Protein: 19 g | Sodium: 350 mg | Fiber: 3 g | Carbohydrates: 26 g | Sugar: 9 g

Tempeh Carnitas

Serve up these delicious vegan carnitas in warm corn tortillas.

INGREDIENTS | SERVES 4

1 (13-ounce) package tempeh, cut into thin strips

1 onion, chopped

4 cloves garlic, minced

1 teaspoon cumin

1 teaspoon dried oregano

¼ teaspoon cinnamon

2 cups Vegetable Broth (see Chapter 3)

1 teaspoon salt

¼ teaspoon black pepper

Add all of the ingredients to a 4-quart slow cooker. Cover and cook on high heat for 2–3 hours.

PER SERVING | Calories: 199 | Fat: 9 g | Protein: 17 g | Sodium: 525 mg | Fiber: 1 g | Carbohydrates: 14 g | Sugar: 2 g

CHAPTER 14

Desserts

Easy Applesauce

Homemade applesauce is easy to make and tastes much better than what you can get in the store. It freezes well, too, so you can make extra when apples are in season.

INGREDIENTS | SERVES 6

10 medium apples, peeled, cored, and sliced
2 tablespoons fresh lemon juice
2 tablespoons water
6-inch cinnamon stick (optional)
¾ cup sugar (optional)

Chunky Applesauce

It's easy to change this recipe into a chunky sauce instead. Once the apples are cooked, mash them with a potato masher instead of blending until smooth.

1. In a 4-quart slow cooker, add the apples, lemon juice, water, and cinnamon stick, if using. Stir to mix.

2. Cover and cook on low for 5 hours, or until the apples are soft and tender.

3. Purée the apples in a food processor or blender, use an immersion blender, or press through a food mill or large mesh strainer.

4. While applesauce is still warm, add sugar, if desired. Store covered in the refrigerator for up to 2 weeks or freeze.

PER SERVING (1 CUP) | Calories: 129 | Fat: 0.3 g | Protein: 1 g | Sodium: 1 mg | Fiber: 3.5 g | Carbohydrates: 34 g | Sugar: 27 g

Coconut Rice Pudding

Rice pudding, also referred to as porridge, is eaten around the world in many different forms.

INGREDIENTS | SERVES 8

1 cup white rice

1 quart soymilk

½ cup Earth Balance Original Buttery Spread

2 tablespoons shredded coconut

1 cup sugar

1 teaspoon cinnamon

¼ teaspoon salt

Add all ingredients to a 4-quart slow cooker. Cover and cook on low heat for 6 hours.

PER SERVING | Calories: 357 | Fat: 14 g | Protein: 6 g | Sodium: 137 mg | Fiber: 1.5 g | Carbohydrates: 52 g | Sugar: 30 g

Carrot Cake

Ice this cake with vegan cream cheese frosting, or glaze the cake while it's still warm.

INGREDIENTS | SERVES 8

1½ cups all-purpose flour
½ teaspoon baking soda
1 teaspoon baking powder
¼ teaspoon salt
¾ teaspoon cinnamon
¼ teaspoon ground cloves
⅛ teaspoon freshly grated nutmeg
2 mashed bananas
¾ cup sugar
⅓ cup Earth Balance Original Buttery Spread
¼ cup water
1 cup grated carrots
½ cup chopped walnuts

Carrot Cake Glaze

Repeatedly pierce the top of the cake with a fork. Add ½ cup lemon, orange, or unsweetened pineapple juice; 1 teaspoon freshly grated lemon or orange zest; and 1½ cups sifted powdered sugar to a microwave-safe measuring cup and stir to combine. Microwave on high for 30 seconds. Stir and repeat until sugar is dissolved. Pour evenly over the cake.

1. In a mixing bowl, add the flour, baking soda, baking powder, salt, cinnamon, cloves, and nutmeg. Stir to combine.

2. In a food processor, add the bananas, sugar, and Earth Balance. Process to cream together. Scrape into the flour mixture.

3. Pour in the water and add the grated carrots to the mixing bowl. Stir and fold to combine all ingredients. Fold in the nuts.

4. Treat a 4-quart slow cooker with nonstick spray. Add the carrot cake batter, and use a spatula to spread it evenly in the crock.

5. Cover and cook on low for 2 hours, or until cake is firm in the center.

PER SERVING | Calories: 298 | Fat: 14 g | Protein: 5.5 g | Sodium: 242 mg | Fiber: 1.5 g | Carbohydrates: 40 g | Sugar: 20 g

"Baked" Apples

Serve these lightly spiced apples as a simple dessert or a breakfast treat.

INGREDIENTS | SERVES 6

6 baking apples, cored and halved
½ cup water
1 cinnamon stick
1 knob peeled fresh ginger
1 vanilla bean

Baking with Apples

When baking or cooking, choose apples with firm flesh such as Granny Smith, Jonathan, McIntosh, Cortland, Pink Lady, Pippin, or Winesap. They will be able to hold up to slow cooking times without turning to mush. Leaving the skin on adds fiber.

1. Place the apples in a single layer on the bottom of a 4- or 6-quart slow cooker. Add the water, cinnamon stick, ginger, and vanilla bean.

2. Cover and cook on low for 6–8 hours, or until the apples are tender and easily pierced with a fork.

3. Use a slotted spoon to remove the apples from the insert. Discard the cinnamon stick, ginger, vanilla bean, and water. Serve hot.

PER SERVING | Calories: 77 | Fat: 0.2 g | Protein: 0.5 g | Sodium: 0.6 mg | Fiber: 3 g | Carbohydrates: 20 g | Sugar: 16 g

Peanut Butter Cake

Serve this cake with a drizzling of chocolate sauce on top to make it a peanut butter cup cake.

INGREDIENTS | SERVES 8

1 cup all-purpose flour
1 cup sugar
1 teaspoon baking powder
½ teaspoon baking soda
¾ cup water
½ cup peanut butter
2 tablespoons vegetable oil
1 teaspoon vanilla extract

1. In a medium bowl, mix all the dry ingredients.

2. In another medium bowl, mix all the wet ingredients.

3. Spray slow cooker with nonstick cooking oil.

4. Combine the dry and wet ingredients, and then pour into a 4-quart slow cooker. Cover and cook on medium-high heat for 1–2 hours.

PER SERVING | Calories: 281 | Fat: 11 g | Protein: 5.5 g | Sodium: 214 mg | Fiber: 1.5 g | Carbohydrates: 40 g | Sugar: 26.5 g

Bananas Foster

Bananas Foster is usually made from flambéed bananas served over vanilla ice cream, but as this recipe proves, the bananas can be made in a slow cooker, too.

INGREDIENTS | SERVES 8

1 cup dark corn syrup

2 tablespoons dark rum

½ teaspoon vanilla extract

1 teaspoon cinnamon

¾ cup Earth Balance Original Buttery Spread

½ teaspoon salt

10 bananas, peeled and cut into bite-sized pieces

4 cups vegan vanilla ice cream

1. In a medium bowl, stir in the corn syrup, rum, vanilla extract, cinnamon, Earth Balance, and salt.

2. Add mixture and bananas to a 4-quart slow cooker. Cover and cook on low heat for 1–2 hours. Serve over a scoop of vegan ice cream.

PER SERVING | Calories: 563 | Fat: 25 g | Protein: 4 g | Sodium: 235 mg | Fiber: 4.5 g | Carbohydrates: 83 g | Sugar: 44 g

Banana Bread

Oat bran adds extra fiber to this recipe, making it a heart-healthier bread.

INGREDIENTS | SERVES 8

1½ cups all-purpose flour

½ cup oat bran

¾ cup sugar

¼ teaspoon baking soda

2 teaspoons baking powder

½ teaspoon salt

3 ripe bananas, mashed

6 tablespoons softened Earth Balance Original Buttery Spread

2 teaspoons cornstarch mixed in 2 tablespoons warm water

¼ cup plain vegan yogurt

1 teaspoon vanilla

1¼ cups walnuts

Spiced Banana Bread

For cinnamon-spiced banana bread, in Step 1 add 1 teaspoon ground cinnamon and ¼ teaspoon each of ground cloves, ginger, allspice, and nutmeg to the flour.

1. Add the flour, oat bran, sugar, baking soda, baking powder, and salt to a mixing bowl. Stir to mix.

2. In a food processor, add the bananas, Earth Balance, cornstarch mixture, yogurt, and vanilla. Pulse to cream together.

3. Add the walnuts and flour mixture to the food processor. Pulse to combine and chop the walnuts. Scrape down the sides of the container with a spatula and pulse until mixed.

4. Treat a 4-quart slow cooker with nonstick spray. Add the batter to the slow cooker, using a spatula to spread it evenly across the bottom of the crock.

5. Cover and cook on high for 3 hours, or until a toothpick inserted in the center of the bread comes out clean.

6. Allow to cool uncovered before removing it from the slow cooker.

PER SERVING | Calories: 432 | Fat: 22 g | Protein: 8.5 g | Sodium: 332 mg | Fiber: 4 g | Carbohydrates: 54 g | Sugar: 25 g

Ginger Poached Pears

*Fresh ginger best complements pear flavor, but if you only have ground,
start by adding a smaller amount and then increasing after tasting.*

INGREDIENTS | SERVES 8

5 pears, peeled, cored, and cut into wedges

3 cups water

1 cup white sugar

2 tablespoons minced ginger

1 teaspoon cinnamon

Add all ingredients to a 4-quart slow cooker. Cover and cook on low heat for 4 hours.

PER SERVING | Calories: 157 | Fat: 0 g | Protein: 0.5 g | Sodium: 1 mg | Fiber: 3 g | Carbohydrates: 41 g | Sugar: 35 g

Chocolate Coconut Bars

*Shredded coconut sometimes comes sweetened, but if
you'd like to cut the sugar in this treat, use unsweetened instead.*

INGREDIENTS | SERVES 16

2 (14-ounce) packages semisweet vegan chocolate chips

1 cup shredded coconut

1. Add all ingredients to a 4-quart slow cooker. Cover and cook on low heat for 1 hour, stirring every 15 minutes.

2. With a large spoon, scoop out the chocolate mixture and drop it onto wax paper. Allow to cool for 20–30 minutes.

PER SERVING | Calories: 252 | Fat: 16 g | Protein: 2 g | Sodium: 6 mg | Fiber: 3 g | Carbohydrates: 32 g | Sugar: 27 g

Date and Nut Bars

*Once these bars are completely cooled you can store them
in an airtight container and enjoy as a snack later.*

INGREDIENTS | SERVES 15

1 cup pitted and chopped dates

1 cup cranberries

½ cup almonds

½ cup pecans

1 cup flour

1 cup sugar

1 teaspoon baking powder

¼ cup puréed silken tofu

2 tablespoons Earth Balance Original
Buttery Spread

1 teaspoon vanilla

1. Combine all of the ingredients in a large mixing bowl, then pour into a 4-quart slow cooker that has been prepared with cooking spray. Cover and cook over high heat for 2 hours.

2. Allow to cool slightly, then cut into small bars. Transfer to a wire rack and allow the bars to cool completely.

PER SERVING | Calories: 176 | Fat: 6 g | Protein: 2.5 g | Sodium: 51 mg | Fiber: 2.5 g | Carbohydrates: 30 g | Sugar: 21 g

All about Dates

Dates, which are a fruit, come from a type of palm tree and can be eaten fresh or dried. Dried dates are more common. If you can only find dried dates, be sure to rehydrate them by soaking in water before use.

Pumpkin Pie

Crust is normally on the bottom of a pie,
but this recipe mixes the "crust" in with the filling.

INGREDIENTS | SERVES 8

1 (15-ounce) can plain pumpkin

½ cup Bisquick

¼ cup sugar

¼ cup brown sugar

¾ cup soymilk

½ cup puréed silken tofu

2 teaspoons pumpkin pie spice

1 teaspoon vanilla

1. Combine all of the ingredients in a large mixing bowl, and then transfer to a 4-quart slow cooker that has been prepared with cooking spray.

2. Cover and cook on low heat for 6 hours.

PER SERVING | Calories: 107 | Fat: 1 g | Protein: 3 g | Sodium: 190 mg | Fiber: 1.8 g | Carbohydrates: 23 g | Sugar: 14 g

Chocolate "Mud" Cake

*Slow cooker mud cake might not look pretty,
but the taste more than makes up for it.*

INGREDIENTS | SERVES 8

1 cup flour

½ cup sugar

2 teaspoons baking powder

¼ teaspoon salt

3 tablespoons cocoa powder

3 tablespoons softened Earth Balance Original Buttery Spread

1 teaspoon vanilla

⅓ cup soymilk

½ cup vegan chocolate chips

1 cup vegan chocolate icing

Vegan Chocolate Icing

There are many vegan icings available in your local grocery store, and you might be surprised that they are made by brands such as Duncan Hines and Pillsbury. They are "accidentally vegan" though, which means they aren't advertised as such. Be sure to read the label before buying.

1. In a large mixing bowl, combine the flour, sugar, baking powder, salt, and cocoa powder.

2. In a medium bowl, combine the Earth Balance, vanilla, and soymilk until well blended.

3. Add the wet mixture and the chocolate chips to the large mixing bowl and stir until just combined. Pour the batter into a greased 4-quart slow cooker. Cover and cook on high heat for 2½ hours.

4. Once done, allow the cake to cool slightly, then top with chocolate icing.

PER SERVING | Calories: 388 | Fat: 15 g | Protein: 3.5 g | Sodium: 325 mg | Fiber: 2.5 g | Carbohydrates: 61 g | Sugar: 43 g

Mixed Berry Cobbler

Fresh berries are best for a delicious cobbler, but frozen will work, too.
Just thaw and drain excess water before using them in a recipe.

INGREDIENTS | SERVES 8

1 cup flour
¾ cup sugar, divided
1 teaspoon baking powder
¼ teaspoon cinnamon
¼ teaspoon salt
Egg replacer equivalent to 2 eggs
¼ cup puréed silken tofu
1½ cups chopped strawberries
1½ cups raspberries
1 cup blueberries
1 teaspoon lemon juice

1. In a large bowl, combine the flour, ½ cup sugar, baking powder, cinnamon, and salt, then add the egg replacer and tofu. Stir until well combined.

2. Pour the mixture into a greased 4-quart slow cooker.

3. In a small bowl, combine the remaining ¼ cup sugar, strawberries, raspberries, blueberries, and lemon juice, and then add the berry mixture to the slow cooker. Cover and cook for 2½–3 hours.

PER SERVING | Calories: 174 | Fat: 1 g | Protein: 3 g | Sodium: 150 mg | Fiber: 3 g | Carbohydrates: 38 g | Sugar: 23 g

Poached Figs and Ice Cream

*Poach means to cook in a liquid over high heat,
and it is a wonderful technique to use on delicate figs.*

INGREDIENTS | SERVES 8

15 black mission figs

2 cups port wine

1 cup sugar

1 strip orange zest

½ teaspoon vanilla

2 cinnamon sticks

6 cups vegan vanilla ice cream

1. Add all of the ingredients, except for the ice cream, to a 4-quart slow cooker. Cover and cook on high heat for 3–4 hours.

2. Allow to cool slightly, then serve over a scoop of vanilla ice cream.

PER SERVING | Calories: 350 | Fat: 4.5 g | Protein: 4.5 g | Sodium: 86 mg | Fiber: 1.5 g | Carbohydrates: 67 g | Sugar: 61 g

Vegan Ice Cream

These days there are many options for vegan ice cream in major grocery stores. The most popular types are made from one of three base ingredients—soy, rice milk, or coconut milk—and you should choose one based on your personal preference. Rice-based ice creams tend to have a lighter flavor because the milk is not rich or fatty. Soy ice cream and coconut milk ice cream tend to be richer and smoother.

Spiced Apples and Pears

This bold desert is a great way to warm up on a cold winter night.

INGREDIENTS | SERVES 6

4 apples, peeled, cored, and sliced

4 pears, peeled, cored, and sliced

½ cup Earth Balance Original Buttery Spread

2 tablespoons lemon juice

2 tablespoons vanilla extract

1 cup brown sugar

1 teaspoon cinnamon

Add all ingredients to a 4-quart slow cooker. Cover and cook on low heat for 6 hours.

PER SERVING | Calories: 403 | Fat: 15 g | Protein: 1 g | Sodium: 190 mg | Fiber: 5 g | Carbohydrates: 67 g | Sugar: 57 g

Chocolate Rice Pudding

For an extra chocolaty flavor, try using chocolate soymilk in place of plain in this recipe.

INGREDIENTS | SERVES 4

1 cup white rice

1 quart soymilk

½ cup Earth Balance Original Buttery Spread

1 cup sugar

½ cup vegan chocolate syrup

¼ teaspoon salt

Add all ingredients to a 4-quart slow cooker. Cover and cook on low heat for 6 hours.

PER SERVING | Calories: 664 | Fat: 16 g | Protein: 11 g | Sodium: 394 mg | Fiber: 3 g | Carbohydrates: 119 g | Sugar: 70 g

Chunky Cinnamon Pearsauce

Pears make this dessert an interesting twist on classic applesauce.

INGREDIENTS | SERVES 6

10 pears, peeled, cored, and chopped
1 lemon, juiced
¼ cup water
2 teaspoons cinnamon
¼ cup sugar

1. Add all ingredients to a 4-quart slow cooker. Cover and cook on low heat for 6 hours.

2. Mash the pears with a potato masher and allow to cool. Serve chilled.

PER SERVING | Calories: 197 | Fat: 0.3 g | Protein: 1 g | Sodium: 3 mg | Fiber: 9 g | Carbohydrates: 52 g | Sugar: 35 g

Breakfast

Tofu Frittata

*Frittatas are traditionally made with eggs, but you can use
tofu instead for a cholesterol-free breakfast dish.*

INGREDIENTS | SERVES 4

2 tablespoons olive oil

1 cup peeled and diced red potatoes

½ onion, diced

½ cup diced red pepper

½ cup diced green pepper

1 teaspoon minced jalapeño

1 clove garlic, minced

¼ cup parsley

16 ounces firm tofu

½ cup unsweetened soymilk

4 teaspoons cornstarch

2 tablespoons nutritional yeast

1 teaspoon mustard

½ teaspoon turmeric

1 teaspoon salt

¼ teaspoon black pepper

1. Add the oil to a large pan and sauté the potatoes, onions, peppers, jalapeño, and garlic on medium heat for about 15–20 minutes.

2. Meanwhile, in a blender or food processor, combine the rest of the ingredients until smooth, then pour the mixture into the slow cooker with the potatoes.

3. Cover and cook on high heat for 4 hours, or until the frittata has firmed.

PER SERVING | Calories: 243 | Fat: 12 g | Protein: 14 g | Sodium: 993 mg | Fiber: 5 g | Carbohydrates: 23 g | Sugar: 5 g

Make It a Scramble

To shorten the preparation time for this meal while keeping all of the flavors, try making this dish into a scramble by preparing the entire recipe in the slow cooker. Skip the step of blending the tofu and omit the cornstarch. Add remaining ingredients, breaking apart tofu as you stir, and sauté until cooked through.

Sunrise Tofu Scramble

Go gourmet with this tofu scramble by substituting shiitake mushrooms and Japanese eggplant instead of the broccoli and button mushrooms.

INGREDIENTS | SERVES 4

16 ounces firm tofu, drained and crumbled

½ cup chopped broccoli florets

½ cup sliced button mushrooms

2 tablespoons olive oil

2 teaspoons turmeric

1 teaspoon cumin

¼ teaspoon garlic powder

⅛ teaspoon red pepper flakes

2 cloves garlic, minced

1 teaspoon salt

¼ teaspoon black pepper

½ cup diced tomato,

1 lemon, juiced

2 tablespoons chopped, fresh parsley

1. Add the tofu, broccoli, mushrooms, oil, turmeric, cumin, garlic powder, red pepper flakes, garlic, salt, and black pepper to a 4-quart slow cooker. Cover and cook on low heat for 4 hours.

2. Add the tomatoes, lemon juice, and parsley to the scramble and serve.

PER SERVING | Calories: 146 | Fat: 10 g | Protein: 8.5 g | Sodium: 636 mg | Fiber: 1 g | Carbohydrates: 6 g | Sugar: 2.5 g

Tofu Ranchero

Bring Mexican cuisine to the breakfast table with an easy tofu ranchero.

INGREDIENTS | SERVES 4

3 tablespoons olive oil

1 (16-ounce) package firm tofu, drained and crumbled

½ onion, diced

2 cloves garlic, minced

1 lemon, juiced

½ teaspoon turmeric

1 teaspoon salt

¼ teaspoon black pepper

1 cup cooked pinto beans

8 corn tortillas

½ cup chipotle salsa

1. Add the olive oil, tofu, onion, garlic, lemon juice, turmeric, salt, black pepper, and pinto beans to a 4-quart slow cooker. Cover and cook on low heat for 4 hours.

2. When the ranchero filling is nearly done, brown the tortillas on both sides in a small sauté pan over medium heat, about 3 minutes on each side.

3. Serve by scooping a little bit of the tofu mixture onto each tortilla and topping with salsa.

PER SERVING | Calories: 354 | Fat: 15 g | Protein: 14 g | Sodium: 889 mg | Fiber: 7 g | Carbohydrates: 42 g | Sugar: 4 g

Choosing Salsa

Salsa comes in many delicious and unique varieties. Most are clearly labeled mild, medium, or hot, but one's interpretation of those words can vary greatly. Chipotle salsa has a deep, earthy spice, but you can also use plain tomato salsa or tomatillo salsa in this recipe.

Tempeh Sausage Scramble

*This nutritious alternative to pork sausage and eggs
will help you start your day off right.*

INGREDIENTS | SERVES 4

1 (13-ounce) package tempeh, crumbled

1 (14-ounce) package extra-firm tofu,
drained and crumbled

1 teaspoon dried sage

2 teaspoons brown sugar

⅛ teaspoon red pepper flakes

⅛ teaspoon dried marjoram

½ cup vegetarian "chicken" broth

1 teaspoon salt

¼ teaspoon black pepper

Add all ingredients to a 4-quart slow cooker. Cover and cook
on low heat for 4 hours.

PER SERVING | Calories: 245 | Fat: 12 g | Protein: 23 g |
Sodium: 623 mg | Fiber: 0 g | Carbohydrates: 13 g | Sugar: 3 g

French Toast Casserole

This recipe is a wonderful way to use bread that is slightly stale.

INGREDIENTS | SERVES 8

12 slices raisin bread

2 teaspoons cornstarch mixed in 2 tablespoons water

1 cup soymilk

1 teaspoon vanilla

2 tablespoons dark brown sugar

1 teaspoon cinnamon

¼ teaspoon nutmeg

1. Spray a 4-quart slow cooker with nonstick spray. Layer the bread in the slow cooker.

2. In a small bowl, whisk the cornstarch mixture, soymilk, vanilla, brown sugar, cinnamon, and nutmeg. Pour over the bread.

3. Cover and cook on low for 6–8 hours.

4. Remove the lid and cook uncovered for 30 minutes, or until the liquid has evaporated.

PER SERVING | Calories: 134 | Fat: 2 g | Protein: 4 g | Sodium: 162 mg | Fiber: 2 g | Carbohydrates: 24 g | Sugar: 5.5 g

Breakfast Tofu and Veggies

Nutritional yeast has a cheesy flavor and should not be replaced with other types of yeast.

INGREDIENTS | SERVES 4

¼ cup olive oil

1 (16-ounce) package extra-firm tofu, drained and cubed

½ onion, diced

1 cup chopped broccoli

½ green bell pepper, chopped

½ medium zucchini, chopped

½ cup chopped yellow squash

3 tablespoons soy sauce

¼ cup nutritional yeast

1. Add the oil, tofu, vegetables, and soy sauce to a 4-quart slow cooker and stir until well combined. Cover and cook on low heat for 4 hours.

2. About 1 minute before the tofu and veggies are almost finished, stir in the nutritional yeast and serve.

PER SERVING | Calories: 300 | Fat: 18 g | Protein: 23 g | Sodium: 1,473 mg | Fiber: 2.5 g | Carbohydrates: 12 g | Sugar: 5 g

Onion, Pepper, and Potato Hash

Use a cheese grater to achieve finely grated potatoes for this dish.

INGREDIENTS | SERVES 4

2 tablespoons olive oil

4 cups peeled and grated russet potatoes

½ onion, diced

1 poblano pepper, cored and diced

2 cloves garlic, minced

1 teaspoon chili powder

½ teaspoon paprika

½ teaspoon cumin

1 teaspoon salt

¼ teaspoon pepper

Add all ingredients to a 4-quart slow cooker. Cover and cook on high heat for 4 hours.

PER SERVING | Calories: 190 | Fat: 7 g | Protein: 3.5 g | Sodium: 604 mg | Fiber: 2.5 g | Carbohydrates: 30 g | Sugar: 1.5 g

Better Hash Browns

After you have grated the potatoes for the hash browns, make sure to rinse them in a colander to get rid of the extra starch. Then, allow the potatoes to dry so they will get extra crispy in the slow cooker.

Spicy Breakfast Burrito

*Tofu is a great alternative to eggs in breakfast dishes,
and tofu is naturally cholesterol free!*

INGREDIENTS | SERVES 4

2 tablespoons olive oil

1 (16-ounce) package firm tofu, drained and crumbled

¼ cup diced red onion

1 tablespoon minced jalapeño

¼ cup diced red bell pepper

¼ cup diced poblano pepper

1 cup cooked black beans, drained

2 teaspoons turmeric

1 teaspoon cumin

½ teaspoon chili powder

½ teaspoon salt

¼ teaspoon black pepper

4 flour tortillas

1 avocado, peeled and sliced

½ cup diced tomatoes

¼ cup chopped cilantro

½ cup chipotle salsa

1. Add olive oil, tofu, onion, jalapeño, red bell pepper, and poblano pepper to a 4-quart slow cooker. Sauté on medium-high heat for 5–8 minutes.

2. Add the black beans, turmeric, cumin, chili powder, salt, and black pepper. Cover and cook on low heat for 4 hours.

3. Scoop the filling onto the tortillas and add the avocado, tomato, cilantro, and salsa. Fold the sides of the tortilla in and roll up the burrito.

PER SERVING | Calories: 385 | Fat: 20 g | Protein: 16 g | Sodium: 325 mg | Fiber: 10 g | Carbohydrates: 38 g | Sugar: 5 g

Steaming Tortillas

For best results, steam tortillas on the stovetop using a steamer basket. If you're in a hurry, throw the tortillas into the microwave one at a time and heat for about 30 seconds.

Easy Tofu "Eggs"

Tofu "eggs" are a great form of protein and taste delicious.
Build upon this basic recipe to create a variety of tofu scrambles.

INGREDIENTS | SERVES 4

2 tablespoons olive oil

1 (16-ounce) package firm tofu, drained and crumbled

¼ cup diced onion

2 cloves garlic, minced

1 teaspoon turmeric

½ teaspoon salt

¼ teaspoon black pepper

1 lemon, juiced

1. Add all ingredients, except for the lemon juice, to a 4-quart slow cooker. Cover and cook on low heat for 3–4 hours.

2. About 3 minutes before the "eggs" are almost finished, stir in the lemon juice.

PER SERVING | Calories: 137 | Fat: 9 g | Protein: 8 g | Sodium: 336 mg | Fiber: 0.5 g | Carbohydrates: 4.5 g | Sugar: 1.5 g

Grandma's Cornmeal Mush

This recipe cooks into a thick cornmeal porridge and makes for a tasty yet inexpensive breakfast food.

INGREDIENTS | SERVES 4

2 cups yellow cornmeal

8 cups water

1 teaspoon salt

2 tablespoons Earth Balance Original Buttery Spread

1. Add all ingredients to a 4-quart slow cooker. Cover and cook on low heat for 4 hours.

2. Allow the mush to cool slightly before serving.

PER SERVING | Calories: 305 | Fat: 7 g | Protein: 5 g | Sodium: 609 mg | Fiber: 2.5 g | Carbohydrates: 54 g | Sugar: 1 g

Serving Suggestions

Cornmeal-based dishes are usually served differently depending on what part of the country you live in. In the north and Midwest, it's most likely to be served up sweet and topped with syrup or sugar, but in the South it's usually accompanied by heaping scoops of butter and cheese.

Cranberry and Figs Oatmeal

*Oatmeal is a great source of fiber, but be careful
not to add too many spoonfuls of sugar!*

INGREDIENTS | SERVES 4

2¼ cups water

1½ cups old-fashioned rolled oats

1 tablespoon brown sugar

1 teaspoon sugar

½ teaspoon cinnamon

¼ cup chopped frozen cranberries

¼ cup chopped figs

¼ teaspoon salt

Place all ingredients in a 4-quart slow cooker. Cover and cook on high 1–2 hours, or until the water is absorbed.

PER SERVING | Calories: 159 | Fat: 2 g | Protein: 4 g | Sodium: 115 mg | Fiber: 4 g | Carbohydrates: 31 g | Sugar: 9 g

Homemade Granola

Unlike most slow cooker recipes, this one calls for cooking with the lid off in order to dry out the granola. You don't want to use oats that are too liquidy.

INGREDIENTS | SERVES 8

5 cups old-fashioned rolled oats
1 cup slivered almonds
¼ cup agave nectar
¼ cup canola oil
1 teaspoon vanilla
¼ cup unsweetened flaked coconut
1½ cups cashews
1½ cups raisins

Storage Suggestions

To cool granola faster, put a piece of wax paper on a countertop or baking sheet, and spread the granola over wax paper. . Once cool and completely dry, place it in an airtight container and store for up to 1 month.

1. Place the oats and almonds into a 4-quart slow cooker. Drizzle with agave nectar, oil, and vanilla. Stir the mixture to distribute the syrup evenly.

2. Cook on high, uncovered, for 1½ hours, stirring every 15–20 minutes.

3. Add the coconut, cashews, and raisins, and reduce the heat to low. Cook for 2 hours, stirring every 20 minutes. Allow the granola to cool completely before serving.

PER SERVING | Calories: 555 | Fat: 27 g | Protein: 13.5 g | Sodium: 9 mg | Fiber: 9 g | Carbohydrates: 73 g | Sugar: 27 g

Mixed-Berry Quinoa

Quinoa is an excellent source of vegan protein and fiber, and it's tasty, too!

INGREDIENTS | SERVES 6

2 cups quinoa

4 cups water

2 teaspoons brown sugar

1 teaspoon dried ginger

½ teaspoon cinnamon

⅛ teaspoon nutmeg

1 cup sliced strawberries

1 cup blueberries

1. Place all ingredients, except the berries, into a 4-quart slow cooker. Cover and cook on low heat for 2–3 hours, or until the quinoa is fully cooked.

2. When the quinoa is finished, mix in the berries and serve.

PER SERVING | Calories: 237 | Fat: 3.5 g | Protein: 8 g | Sodium: 8 mg | Fiber: 5 g | Carbohydrates: 43 g | Sugar: 5 g

Home Fries

Home fries are traditionally made in a pan or skillet on the stovetop, but they can be easily adapted for the slow cooker.

INGREDIENTS | SERVES 6

2 pounds red potatoes, peeled and chopped

1 onion, chopped

1 green bell pepper, chopped

2 tablespoons olive oil

½ teaspoon cumin

2 teaspoons paprika

1 teaspoon chili powder

1 teaspoon salt

¼ teaspoon black pepper

Place all ingredients in a 4-quart slow cooker. Cover and cook on high 2 hours.

PER SERVING | Calories: 159 | Fat: 5 g | Protein: 3 g | Sodium: 392 mg | Fiber: 3.5 g | Carbohydrates: 27 g | Sugar: 2 g

Cinnamon Apple Oatmeal

Allspice may sound like a combination of spices, but it's actually just one spice made from the Pimenta dioica plant.

INGREDIENTS | SERVES 4

2¼ cups water

1½ cups old-fashioned rolled oats

1 tablespoon brown sugar

1 teaspoon sugar

½ teaspoon cinnamon

¼ teaspoon allspice

2 apples, peeled and diced

Place all ingredients in a 4-quart slow cooker. Cover and cook on high 1–2 hours, or until the water is absorbed.

PER SERVING | Calories: 171 | Fat: 2 g | Protein: 4 g | Sodium: 7 mg | Fiber: 4 g | Carbohydrates: 35 g | Sugar: 12 g

Savory Red Pepper Grits

*Grits are a true Southern staple, but this recipe has a slight twist
and calls for vegetable broth and red pepper flakes.*

INGREDIENTS | SERVES 6

2 cups stone-ground grits

3 cups water

3 cups Vegetable Broth (see Chapter 3)

2 tablespoons Earth Balance Original
Buttery Spread

1 teaspoon red pepper flakes

1 teaspoon salt

¼ teaspoon black pepper

Place all ingredients in a 4-quart slow cooker. Cover and
cook on high 2 hours.

PER SERVING | Calories: 230 | Fat: 4.5 g | Protein: 5 g |
Sodium: 423 mg | Fiber: 3 g | Carbohydrates: 44 g | Sugar: 1.5 g

Choosing Grits

You may be most familiar with instant or
fast-cooking grits, but those should be
avoided in slow cooker recipes. Choose
stone-ground or whole-kernel grits instead,
which will hold up better during the long
cook time.

Tempeh Bacon Bake

*The combination of soy sauce, liquid smoke, and brown sugar are
what help give the tempeh a fake bacon flavor in this dish.*

INGREDIENTS | SERVES 6

1 (13-ounce) package tempeh, cut into bite-size pieces

2 tablespoons soy sauce

1 teaspoon liquid smoke

2 tablespoons apple cider vinegar

1 tablespoon brown sugar

2 pounds red potatoes, peeled and chopped

2 cups diced tomatoes

1 onion, chopped

1 green bell pepper, chopped

1 teaspoon salt

¼ teaspoon black pepper

Place all ingredients in a 4-quart slow cooker. Cover and cook on high 2 hours.

PER SERVING | Calories: 256 | Fat: 7 g | Protein: 15 g | Sodium: 612 mg | Fiber: 4 g | Carbohydrates: 37 g | Sugar: 6.5 g

Brunch Spinach

*While reminiscent of creamed spinach, this vegan version isn't
an exact match, so be prepared for something a little different.*

INGREDIENTS | SERVES 6

4 cups frozen spinach, thawed

1 cup silken tofu

1 cup unsweetened soymilk

1 teaspoon Dijon mustard

¼ cup nutritional flakes

1 teaspoon turmeric

1 teaspoon cup soy sauce

1 teaspoon salt

¼ teaspoon black pepper

Place all ingredients in a 4-quart slow cooker. Cover and cook on low heat for 3 hours. Serve as a side dish with a savory brunch entrée, such as a frittata.

PER SERVING | Calories: 85 | Fat: 2 g | Protein: 10 g | Sodium: 510 mg | Fiber: 4 g | Carbohydrates: 8 g | Sugar: 1 g

Vegan Migas

Serve this breakfast dish just as you would many other Tex-Mex dishes: taco-style in a tortilla!

INGREDIENTS | SERVES 4

2 cups slightly crumbled tortilla chips

2 cups silken tofu

1 cup unsweetened soymilk

1 teaspoon Dijon mustard

¼ cup nutritional yeast flakes

1 teaspoon turmeric

2 tablespoons soy sauce

1 teaspoon salt

¼ teaspoon black pepper

Place all ingredients in a 4-quart slow cooker. Cover and cook on high 2 hours.

PER SERVING | Calories: 225 | Fat: 9 g | Protein: 12 g | Sodium: 989 mg | Fiber: 2 g | Carbohydrates: 22 g | Sugar: 2 g

Tex-Mex Migas

Tex-Mex migas, like this recipe, are slightly different than other versions with the same name. It's usually made with eggs and crumbled tortillas chips, while other versions are a bread-based breakfast dish.

Jalapeño Hash Browns

*The type of jalapeños you choose for this dish can make the heat vary greatly,
so be careful if you don't like it hot.*

INGREDIENTS | SERVES 6

2 tablespoons olive oil

2 pounds red potatoes, peeled and shredded

1 onion, diced

¼ cup chopped pickled jalapeños

1 teaspoon salt

¼ teaspoon black pepper

Place all ingredients in a 4-quart slow cooker. Cover and cook on high 2 hours.

PER SERVING | Calories: 152 | Fat: 4.7 g | Protein: 3 g | Sodium: 402 mg | Fiber: 3 g | Carbohydrates: 25 g | Sugar: 2.4 g

CHAPTER 16

Beverages

White Tea–Berry Fusion

Fruit-filled teas are delicious served warm or chilled over ice.

INGREDIENTS | SERVES 8

8 white tea bags
½ cup halved blackberries
½ cup halved raspberries
2 tablespoons sugar
8 cups water

1. Add all ingredients to a 4-quart slow cooker. Cover and cook on low heat for 2 hours.

2. Remove the tea bags and strain the fruit before serving.

PER SERVING | Calories: 22 | Fat: 0 g | Protein: 0.4 g | Sodium: 9 mg | Fiber: 1 g | Carbohydrates: 5 g | Sugar: 3 g

White Tea

White tea is harvested mainly in China. It is made from immature tea leaves plucked just before the buds fully open. The leaves go through even less processing than green tea leaves (they are steamed rather than air dried). Because of this, they remain close to their natural state, meaning they contain more cancer-fighting polyphenols than other teas.

Ginger-Pear Punch

Adding a touch of sparkling water at the end will make this punch even more refreshing.

INGREDIENTS | SERVES 6

6 cups water

½ cup sugar

1-inch piece fresh ginger, peeled and grated

6 pears, peeled and diced

Ice

24 ounces sparkling water

1. In a 4-quart slow cooker, add the water, sugar, and ginger.

2. Place the pears in a cheesecloth and twist to close, then add to the slow cooker.

3. Cover and cook on low heat for 3 hours.

4. Allow the punch to cool completely, then fill each glass with ice, ¾ full with the punch, and top it off with a splash of plain sparkling water.

PER SERVING | Calories: 162 | Fat: 0.2 g | Protein: 0.5 g | Sodium: 2 mg | Fiber: 5 g | Carbohydrates: 42 g | Sugar: 33 g

Fruit Punch

You can try a variety of different fruits in this versatile punch.

INGREDIENTS | SERVES 6

1 cup strawberries
3 oranges, halved
1 cup pitted and chopped cherries
1 cup chopped grapes
½ cup sugar
2 quarts water

1. Add all ingredients to a 4-quart slow cooker. Cover and cook on low heat for 2 hours.

2. Pour punch through a strainer and serve chilled.

PER SERVING | Calories: 137 | Fat: 0.2 g | Protein: 1.2 g | Sodium: 10 mg | Fiber: 2 g | Carbohydrates: 35 g | Sugar: 31 g

The Origins of Fruit Punch

Fruit punch was introduced to the English by India and is now popular worldwide. The word *punch* is borrowed from the Hindi word *panch*.

Apple Ginger Punch

The ginger gives a little more oomph to this punch.

INGREDIENTS | SERVES 6

6 apples, peeled and diced

1-inch piece fresh ginger, peeled and grated

6 cups water

½ cup sugar

Ice

24 ounces sparkling water

1. Add all ingredients to a 4-quart slow cooker. Cover and cook on low heat for 2 hours.

2. Pour punch through a strainer and allow to chill.

3. To serve, fill each glass with ice, ¾ full with the punch, and then top it off with a splash of sparkling water.

PER SERVING | Calories: 142 | Fat: 0.2 g | Protein: 0.4 g | Sodium: 10 mg | Fiber: 2 g | Carbohydrates: 37 g | Sugar: 33 g

Hot Chocolate

If you can't find chocolate chips, chocolate syrup works just as well.

INGREDIENTS | SERVES 6

8 cups soymilk
½ cup vegan chocolate chips

1. Pour the soymilk and vegan chocolate chips into a 4-quart slow cooker.

2. Cover and cook on low heat for 1 hour. Serve warm.

PER SERVING | Calories: 174 | Fat: 9 g | Protein: 10 g | Sodium: 114 mg | Fiber: 2 g | Carbohydrates: 14 g | Sugar: 9 g

The Arnold Palmer

The Arnold Palmer is a refreshing beverage served on golf courses in the South, but it's popularity has spread in recent years.

INGREDIENTS | SERVES 6

8 bags black tea

2 quarts water

¾ cup sugar

6 lemons, cut in half

1. Add all ingredients to a 4-quart slow cooker. Cover and cook on low heat for 2 hours.

2. Pour the drink through a strainer and allow to cool. Serve chilled.

PER SERVING | Calories: 114 | Fat: 0 g | Protein: 0.6 g | Sodium: 10 mg | Fiber: 1.6 g | Carbohydrates: 30 g | Sugar: 26 g

Who Invented the Arnold Palmer?

Although there are many different versions of the story, golf legend Arnold Palmer claims that he is the one who first created this refreshing summertime drink. The drink consists of one part lemonade, one part tea.

Cherry Limeade

Nothing says summer like a homemade limeade.

INGREDIENTS | SERVES 6

2 cups frozen cherries
10 limes, cut in half
½ cup sugar
2 quarts water

1. Add all ingredients to a 4-quart slow cooker. Cover and cook on low heat for 2 hours.

2. Pour the cherry limeade through a strainer and allow to cool. Serve chilled.

PER SERVING | Calories: 122 | Fat: 0.4 g | Protein: 1.2 g | Sodium: 12 mg | Fiber: 3 g | Carbohydrates: 34 g | Sugar: 23 g

Vanilla-Lavender Tea

Black tea, green tea, or white tea will all work well in this recipe. The choice is yours!

INGREDIENTS | SERVES 8

8 black tea bags
8 cups water
½ teaspoon vanilla extract
1 tablespoon sugar
2 sprigs lavender

1. Place the tea bags, water, vanilla extract, and sugar in a 4-quart slow cooker.

2. Place the lavender in a cheesecloth and twist to close, then add to the slow cooker.

3. Cover and cook on low heat for 2 hours.

4. Remove the tea bags and lavender before serving the tea warm.

PER SERVING | Calories: 7 | Fat: 0 g | Protein: 0g | Sodium: 7 g | Fiber: 0 g | Carbohydrates: 1.5 g | Sugar: 1.5 g

Orange and Blackberry Punch

If blackberries aren't in season, feel free to use frozen instead.

INGREDIENTS | SERVES 6

1 cup blackberries

6 oranges, cut in half

1 lemon, cut in half

½ cup sugar

2 quarts water

1. Add all ingredients to a 4-quart slow cooker. Cover and cook on low heat for 2 hours.

2. Pour punch through a strainer and serve chilled.

PER SERVING | Calories: 139 | Fat: 0.3 g | Protein: 1.5 g | Sodium: 0.6 mg | Fiber: 4 g | Carbohydrates: 35 g | Sugar: 30 g

More Reasons to Eat Blackberries

Blackberries are loaded with antioxidants. These antioxidants give the berry its dark purple color and have been proven to assist in memory retention.

Orange-Mint Green Tea

This tea is subtle and refreshing. Enjoy it warm or chilled over ice.

INGREDIENTS | SERVES 6

6 oranges, cut in half
8 bags green tea
¼ cup whole mint leaves
½ cup sugar
¼ cup agave nectar
2 quarts water

1. Add all ingredients to a 4-quart slow cooker. Cover and cook on low heat for 2 hours.

2. Pour the tea through a strainer.

PER SERVING | Calories: 172 | Fat: 0.2 g | Protein: 1.4 g | Sodium: 4 mg | Fiber: 3 g | Carbohydrates: 44 g | Sugar: 40 g

Agave Green Tea

Ginger has been proven to help with gastrointestinal problems.

INGREDIENTS | SERVES 6

8 bags green tea

2 quarts water

½ cup agave nectar

1-inch piece ginger, peeled and chopped

1. Add all ingredients to a 4-quart slow cooker. Cover and cook on low heat for 2 hours.

2. Pour the tea through a strainer.

PER SERVING | Calories: 85 | Fat: 0 g | Protein: 0 g | Sodium: 10 mg | Fiber: 0 g | Carbohydrates: 23 g | Sugar: 23 g

Blackberry-Mint Iced Tea

Not only is mint delicious, it contains good amounts of vitamins A and C.

INGREDIENTS | SERVES 6

8 bags black tea
2 quarts water
¾ cup sugar
1 cup blackberries
¼ cup whole mint leaves

Cancer-Fighting Mint

Mint has been found to reduce the risk of colon and rectal cancer. It protects the body against cancerous cell growth.

1. Add all ingredients to a 4-quart slow cooker. Cover and cook on low heat for 2 hours.

2. Pour the tea through a strainer and allow to cool. Serve chilled.

PER SERVING | Calories: 107 | Fat: 0 g | Protein: 0 g | Sodium: 9 mg | Fiber: 1 g | Carbohydrates: 27 g | Sugar: 26 g

Apple Cider

To spike this cider, try adding 6 ounces of rum.

INGREDIENTS | SERVES 6

2 quarts apple cider

½ cup brown sugar

¼ cup agave nectar

2 oranges, halved

2 cinnamon sticks, left whole

1. Add all ingredients to a 4-quart slow cooker. Cover and cook on low heat for 2 hours.

2. Pour the cider through a strainer.

PER SERVING | Calories: 285 | Fat: 0.4 g | Protein: 0.8 g | Sodium: 18 mg | Fiber: 1.5 g | Carbohydrates: 72 g | Sugar: 65 g

Lemonade

Add 6 ounces of vodka to make this a hard lemonade.

INGREDIENTS | SERVES 6

10 lemons, halved

2 quarts water

½ cup sugar

1. Add all ingredients to a 4-quart slow cooker. Cover and cook on low heat for 2 hours.

2. Pour the lemonade through a strainer and allow to cool. Serve chilled.

PER SERVING | Calories: 93 | Fat: 0 g | Protein: 1 g | Sodium: 11 mg | Fiber: 2.5 g | Carbohydrates: 25 g | Sugar: 19 g

Strawberry Lemonade

*If fresh strawberries aren't in season or if they're just too expensive,
use frozen strawberries instead.*

INGREDIENTS | SERVES 6

10 lemons, cut in half
1 cup strawberries
2 quarts water
½ cup sugar

Growing Strawberries

Strawberries are an easy plant to grow in
your home garden. The best time to plant
is early to middle spring.

1. Add all ingredients to a 4-quart slow cooker. Cover and cook on low heat for 2 hours.

2. Pour the strawberry lemonade through a strainer and allow to cool. Serve chilled.

PER SERVING | Calories: 100 | Fat: 0.3 g | Protein: 1 g |
Sodium: 11 mg | Fiber: 3 g | Carbohydrates: 27 g | Sugar: 20 g

Mulled Wine

This wine punch is great for the holidays.

INGREDIENTS | SERVES 6

1 bottle (750 milliliters) red wine

2 cinnamon sticks

½ cup agave nectar

1 teaspoon allspice

2 oranges, cut in half

2 lemons, cut in half

Add all ingredients to a 4-quart slow cooker. Cover and cook on low heat for 2 hours. Serve warm.

PER SERVING | Calories: 217 | Fat: 0 g | Protein: 1 g | Sodium: 6 mg | Fiber: 1.5 g | Carbohydrates: 33 g | Sugar: 28 g

Cranberry-Apple Punch

Cranberries are mainly found in the northern United States and Canada.

INGREDIENTS | SERVES 8

6 apples, peeled and diced
8 cups cranberry juice
1 lemon, halved
1½ quarts water
¾ cup sugar

1. Add all ingredients to a 4-quart slow cooker. Cover and cook on low heat for 2 hours.

2. Pour the punch through a strainer and allow to cool. Serve chilled.

PER SERVING | Calories: 249 | Fat: 0.5 g | Protein: 1.3 g | Sodium: 10 mg | Fiber: 2 g | Carbohydrates: 65 g | Sugar: 61 g

Strawberry-Mint White Tea

*White tea has been found to bolster the immune system,
so this drink is not only delicious, it's good for you, too!*

INGREDIENTS | SERVES 6

8 bags white tea

2 quarts water

½ cup sugar

1 cup chopped strawberries

¼ cup whole mint leaves

1. Add all ingredients to a 4-quart slow cooker. Cover and cook on low heat for 2 hours.

2. Pour the tea through a strainer and serve warm.

PER SERVING | Calories: 75 | Fat: 0 g | Protein: 0.3 g | Sodium: 13 mg | Fiber: 0.7 g | Carbohydrates: 19 g | Sugar: 17 g

The Origins of White Tea

According to Chinese legend, white tea originated when an emperor was unable to find clean water while traveling through the Chinese countryside. He ordered the water to be boiled before he would drink it, at which point a white tea leaf fell into the water and was allowed to steep.

Cranberry Black Tea

Black tea is stronger and contains more caffeine than both green and white tea.

INGREDIENTS | SERVES 6

8 bags black tea
1½ quarts water
½ cup sugar
2 cups cranberry juice

1. Add all ingredients to a 4-quart slow cooker. Cover and cook on low heat for 2 hours.

2. Pour the tea through a strainer and serve warm.

PER SERVING | Calories: 103 | Fat: 0 g | Protein: 0.3 g | Sodium: 8 mg | Fiber: 0 g | Carbohydrates: 27 g | Sugar: 26 g

Apple Pie Punch

This cold-weather drink is basically a healthy dessert in a cup.

INGREDIENTS | SERVES 6

6 apples, peeled and diced
4 cups apple cider
1 cup frozen cherries
3 oranges, halved
½ cup sugar

1. Add all ingredients to a 4-quart slow cooker. Cover and cook on low heat for 2 hours.

2. Pour the punch through a strainer and allow to cool. Serve chilled.

PER SERVING | Calories: 261 | Fat: 0.5 g | Protein: 1 g | Sodium: 7 mg | Fiber: 3 g | Carbohydrates: 63 g | Sugar: 54 g

Mandarin Orange and Mint White Tea

China produces over half of the world's mandarin oranges.

INGREDIENTS | SERVES 6

8 bags white tea

2 quarts water

1 cup chopped mandarin oranges

¼ cup whole mint leaves

Mandarin Oranges

Just one mandarin orange can provide up to 80 percent of the recommended vitamin C requirements for the body. They are also packed with antioxidants.

1. Add all ingredients to a 4-quart slow cooker. Cover and cook on low heat for 2 hours.

2. Pour the tea through a strainer and serve warm.

PER SERVING | Calories: 20 | Fat: 0 g | Protein: 0.5 g | Sodium: 13 mg | Fiber: 1 g | Carbohydrates: 4 g | Sugar: 3 g

Mango and Apricot Punch

The apricot is a member of the plum family.

INGREDIENTS | SERVES 6

1 (15-ounce) can mangos, chopped
1 cup chopped apricots
5 oranges, halved
1 lemon, halved
2 quarts water
½ cup sugar

1. Add all ingredients to a 4-quart slow cooker. Cover and cook on low heat for 2 hours.

2. Pour the punch through a strainer and allow to cool. Serve chilled.

PER SERVING | Calories: 177 | Fat: 0.5 g | Protein: 2 g | Sodium: 11 mg | Fiber: 3 g | Carbohydrates: 45 g | Sugar: 39 g

Cinnamon Roll in a Cup

This is a great evening cocktail to serve in the winter. There's no need to make dessert if you're having this sweet treat!

INGREDIENTS | SERVES 6

6 cups apple cider

2 cups water

½ cup brown sugar

1 tablespoon cinnamon

½ cup maple syrup

½ cup sugar

3 oranges, halved

1. Add all ingredients to a 4-quart slow cooker. Cover and cook on low heat for 2 hours.

2. Pour the drink through a strainer.

PER SERVING | Calories: 352 | Fat: 0.5 g | Protein: 1 g | Sodium: 20 mg | Fiber: 2.5 g | Carbohydrates: 89 g | Sugar: 80 g

Strawberry and Orange Punch

Look for fresh, local strawberries from June through August.

INGREDIENTS | SERVES 6

5 oranges, halved

1 cup chopped strawberries

2 quarts water

½ cup sugar

1. Add all ingredients to a 4-quart slow cooker. Cover and cook on low heat for 2 hours.

2. Pour the punch through a strainer and allow to cool. Serve chilled.

PER SERVING | Calories: 124 | Fat: 0 g | Protein: 1 g | Sodium: 10 mg | Fiber: 2 g | Carbohydrates: 31 g | Sugar: 28 g

Praise for the Orange

Oranges are one of the most popular fruits in the world. They are loaded with vitamin C and antioxidants, and provide immune support for the body.

Mango Mint Punch

The mango originated in India, but it has spread in popularity throughout the world.

INGREDIENTS | SERVES 6

1 (15-ounce) can mangos, chopped
1 cup frozen cherries
2 quarts water
½ cup sugar
¼ cup whole mint leaves

1. Add all ingredients to a 4-quart slow cooker. Cover and cook on low heat for 2 hours.

2. Pour the punch through a strainer and allow to cool. Serve chilled.

PER SERVING | Calories: 125 | Fat: 0 g | Protein: 1 g | Sodium: 14 mg | Fiber: 2 g | Carbohydrates: 32 g | Sugar: 28 g

Glossary of Terms and Ingredients

braising

A cooking method that consists of browning a protein or vegetable, then simmering it in liquid to finish cooking it.

caponata

A popular Italian dish made with eggplant and tomato.

coulis

A sauce consisting of puréed vegetables or fruits.

lemongrass

A thick, lemon-scented grass often used in Thai cooking.

masala

An Indian curry that often includes cardamom, coriander, pepper, fennel, and nutmeg.

millet

A vitamin-rich and mildly flavored grain that is commonly used in hot climates.

orzo

A rice-shaped pasta.

paella

A Spanish rice dish seasoned with saffron.

quinoa

A tiny grain, similar to couscous, high in protein and nutrients.

ratatouille

A vegetable stew often consisting of tomatoes, bell peppers, zucchini, squash, and onions.

risotto

An Italian dish prepared by slowly stirring hot stock into rice.

sauté

To fry briefly with a small amount of fat over high heat.

seitan

A meat substitute made from wheat gluten.

tempeh

An Indonesian food made from fermented soybeans and fungus.

tofu

A cheeselike food made from soybeans.

TVP

Texturized vegetable protein, a meat substitute, similar to ground beef, made from soybeans.

Nutritional Content of Vegan Protein Sources

INGREDIENT	PROTEIN (G)	IRON (MG)	CALCIUM (MG)
Soybeans, boiled (1 cup)	28.62	4.5	261
Tempeh, cooked (½ cup)	18.19	2.13	96
Lentils, boiled (1 cup)	17.9	6.59	38
Pinto beans, boiled (1 cup)	15.4	3.57	79
Black beans, boiled (1 cup)	15.2	3.61	46
Chickpeas, boiled (1 cup)	14.5	4.74	80
Tofu, firm (½ cup)	10.32	2.03	253
Soymilk, unfortified (1 cup)	8.0	.2	8
Roasted peanuts (1 ounce)	6.71	.64	15

Source: USDA.gov

Internet Resources

Vegan Information

PETA.org

A comprehensive resource provided by the world's largest animal rights group. Contains information on animal rights, a free vegan starter kit, vegan recipes, cruelty-free shopping guide, "accidentally vegan" shopping list, games, contests, celebrity ads, and more.
www.peta.org

Vegan Online Stores

The Vegan Store

A vegan store that started as a mail-order catalog and is now online. Sells food, clothing, home products, cosmetics, media, and beauty and health-care products.
www.veganstore.com

Food Fight! Vegan Grocery

A Portland, Oregon, vegan food and online store. Sells vegan meats, cheeses, sweets, beverages, and vitamins.
www.foodfightgrocery.com

Recipes

VegWeb.com

Over 13,000 vegetarian recipes and photos provided by registered users. The site also contains forums, a meal planner, articles, and coupons. *www.vegweb.com*

Fat-Free Vegan Recipes

Low-fat and no-fat vegan recipes. The site also contains a popular blog, forum, and additional information on fat-free cooking. *www.fatfreevegan.com*

Post Punk Kitchen

Vegan cooking with an edge. Free recipes, including categories for low-fat, no refined sugar, and wheat free. *www.theppk.com/recipes*

Slow Cookers

A Year of Slow Cooking

In 2008, Stephanie O'Dea made a resolution to use her slow cooker every day for a year; this blog chronicled her journey. The *New York Times* bestselling author continues to release new recipes on her blog. *http://crockpot365.blogspot.com*

Standard U.S./Metric Measurement Conversions

VOLUME CONVERSIONS

U.S. Volume Measure	Metric Equivalent
⅛ teaspoon	0.5 milliliters
¼ teaspoon	1 milliliters
½ teaspoon	2 milliliters
1 teaspoon	5 milliliters
½ tablespoon	7 milliliters
1 tablespoon (3 teaspoons)	15 milliliters
2 tablespoons (1 fluid ounce)	30 milliliters
¼ cup (4 tablespoons)	60 milliliters
⅓ cup	90 milliliters
½ cup (4 fluid ounces)	125 milliliters
⅔ cup	160 milliliters
¾ cup (6 fluid ounces)	180 milliliters
1 cup (16 tablespoons)	250 milliliters
1 pint (2 cups)	500 milliliters
1 quart (4 cups)	1 liter (about)

WEIGHT CONVERSIONS

U.S. Weight Measure	Metric Equivalent
½ ounce	15 grams
1 ounce	30 grams
2 ounces	60 grams
3 ounces	85 grams
¼ pound (4 ounces)	115 grams
½ pound (8 ounces)	225 grams
¾ pound (12 ounces)	340 grams
1 pound (16 ounces)	454 grams

OVEN TEMPERATURE CONVERSIONS

Degrees Fahrenheit	Degrees Celsius
200 degrees F	95 degrees C
250 degrees F	120 degrees C
275 degrees F	135 degrees C
300 degrees F	150 degrees C
325 degrees F	160 degrees C
350 degrees F	180 degrees C
375 degrees F	190 degrees C
400 degrees F	205 degrees C
425 degrees F	220 degrees C
450 degrees F	230 degrees C

BAKING PAN SIZES

American	Metric
8 × 1½ inch round baking pan	20 × 4 cm cake tin
9 × 1½ inch round baking pan	23 × 3.5 cm cake tin
1 × 7 × 1½ inch baking pan	28 × 18 × 4 cm baking tin
13 × 9 × 2 inch baking pan	30 × 20 × 5 cm baking tin
2 quart rectangular baking dish	30 × 20 × 3 cm baking tin
15 × 10 × 2 inch baking pan	30 × 25 × 2 cm baking tin (Swiss roll tin)
9 inch pie plate	22 × 4 or 23 × 4 cm pie plate
7 or 8 inch springform pan	18 or 20 cm springform or loose bottom cake tin
9 × 5 × 3 inch loaf pan	23 × 13 × 7 cm or 2 lb narrow loaf or pate tin
1½ quart casserole	1.5 litre casserole
2 quart casserole	2 litre casserole

Index

Note: Page numbers in **bold** indicate recipe category lists.